Basketball Stat Tracker

Copyright © 2022 BSB SCORE PUBLISHING

Name : --

Phone : --

Address: --

Book Information

Start Date :	End Date :

IF FOUND, PLEASE CONTACT -------------------------------

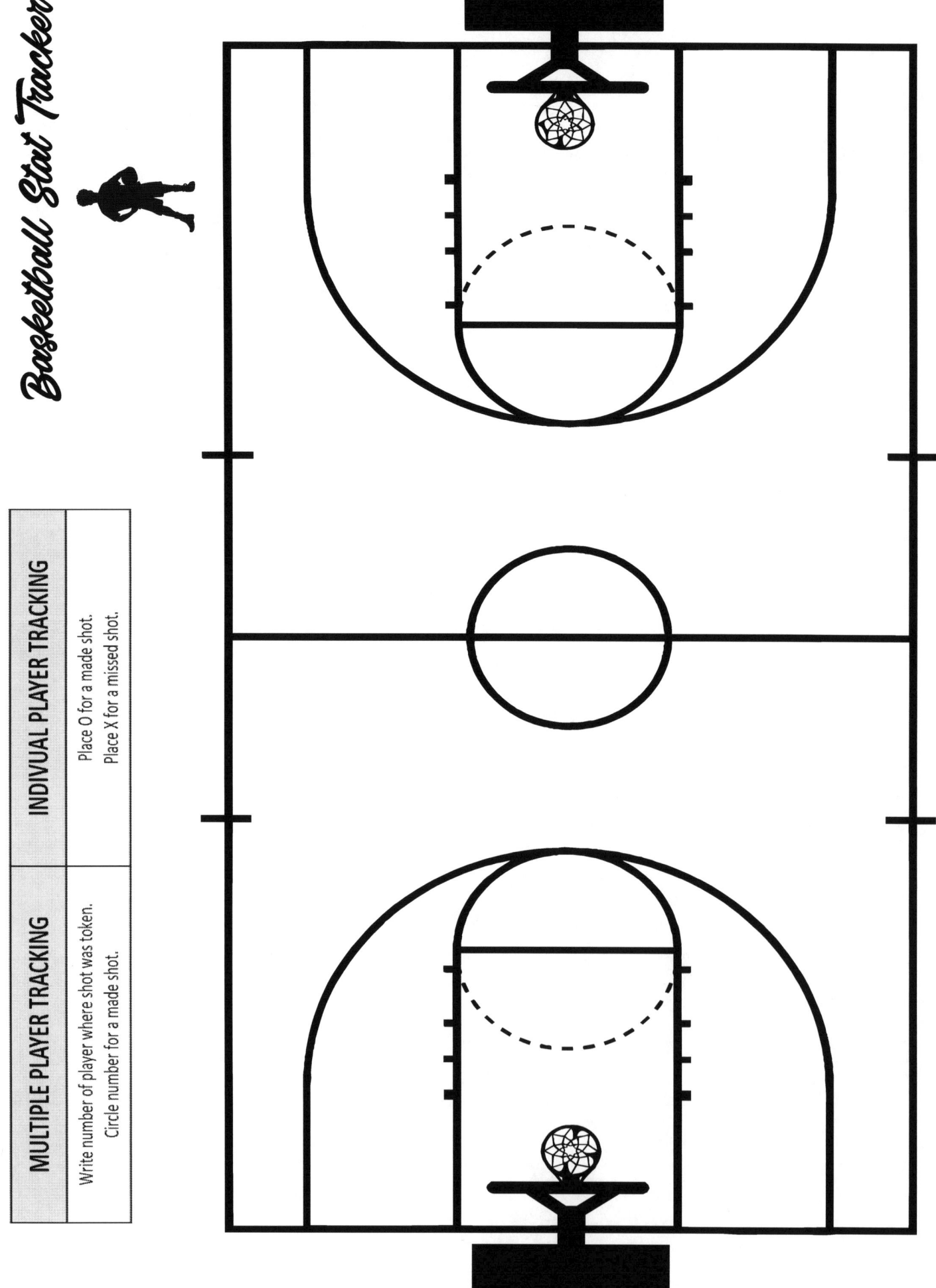

Basketball Stat Tracker

MULTIPLE PLAYER TRACKING	INDIVUAL PLAYER TRACKING
Write number of player where shot was token. Circle number for a made shot.	Place O for a made shot. Place X for a missed shot.

Basketball Stat Tracker

VISITORS	
HOME	
LOCATION	

SCORE	
HALF	
FINAL	

DATE

#	PLAYER	FLS	2-POINT FG		3-POINT FG		FREE THROW		REBOUND		AST	TO	STL	BLK	TOTAL POINTS
			ATT	MADE	ATT	MADE	ATT	MADE	OFF	DEF					
		1 2 3 4 5 1 2													
		1 2 3 4 5 1 2													
		1 2 3 4 5 1 2													
		1 2 3 4 5 1 2													
		1 2 3 4 5 1 2													
		1 2 3 4 5 1 2													
		1 2 3 4 5 1 2													
		1 2 3 4 5 1 2													
		1 2 3 4 5 1 2													
		1 2 3 4 5 1 2													
		1 2 3 4 5 1 2													
		1 2 3 4 5 1 2													
		1 2 3 4 5 1 2													
	TEAM TOTALS														

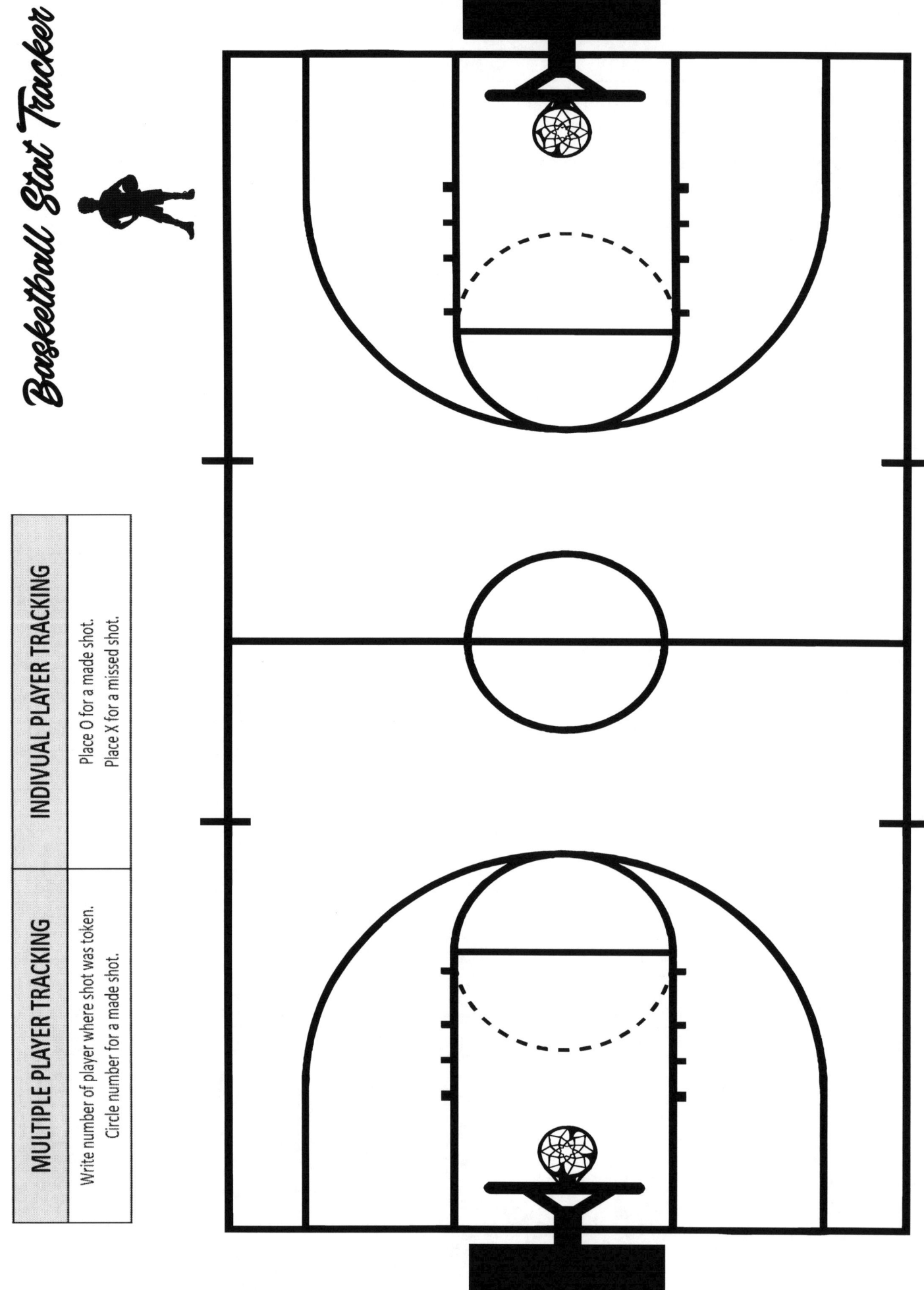

Basketball Stat Tracker

MULTIPLE PLAYER TRACKING	INDIVIUAL PLAYER TRACKING
Write number of player where shot was token.	Place O for a made shot.
Circle number for a made shot.	Place X for a missed shot.

Basketball Stat Tracker

VISITORS	
HOME	
LOCATION	

SCORE	
HALF	
FINAL	

DATE

#	PLAYER	FLS			2-POINT FG		3-POINT FG		FREE THROW		REBOUND		AST	TO	STL	BLK	TOTAL POINTS
					ATT	MADE	ATT	MADE	ATT	MADE	OFF	DEF					
		1 2 3 4 5	1 2														
		1 2 3 4 5	1 2														
		1 2 3 4 5	1 2														
		1 2 3 4 5	1 2														
		1 2 3 4 5	1 2														
		1 2 3 4 5	1 2														
		1 2 3 4 5	1 2														
		1 2 3 4 5	1 2														
		1 2 3 4 5	1 2														
		1 2 3 4 5	1 2														
		1 2 3 4 5	1 2														
		1 2 3 4 5	1 2														
		1 2 3 4 5	1 2														
		1 2 3 4 5	1 2														
	TEAM TOTALS																

Basketball Stat Tracker

MULTIPLE PLAYER TRACKING

Write number of player where shot was token.

Circle number for a made shot.

INDIVUAL PLAYER TRACKING

Place O for a made shot.

Place X for a missed shot.

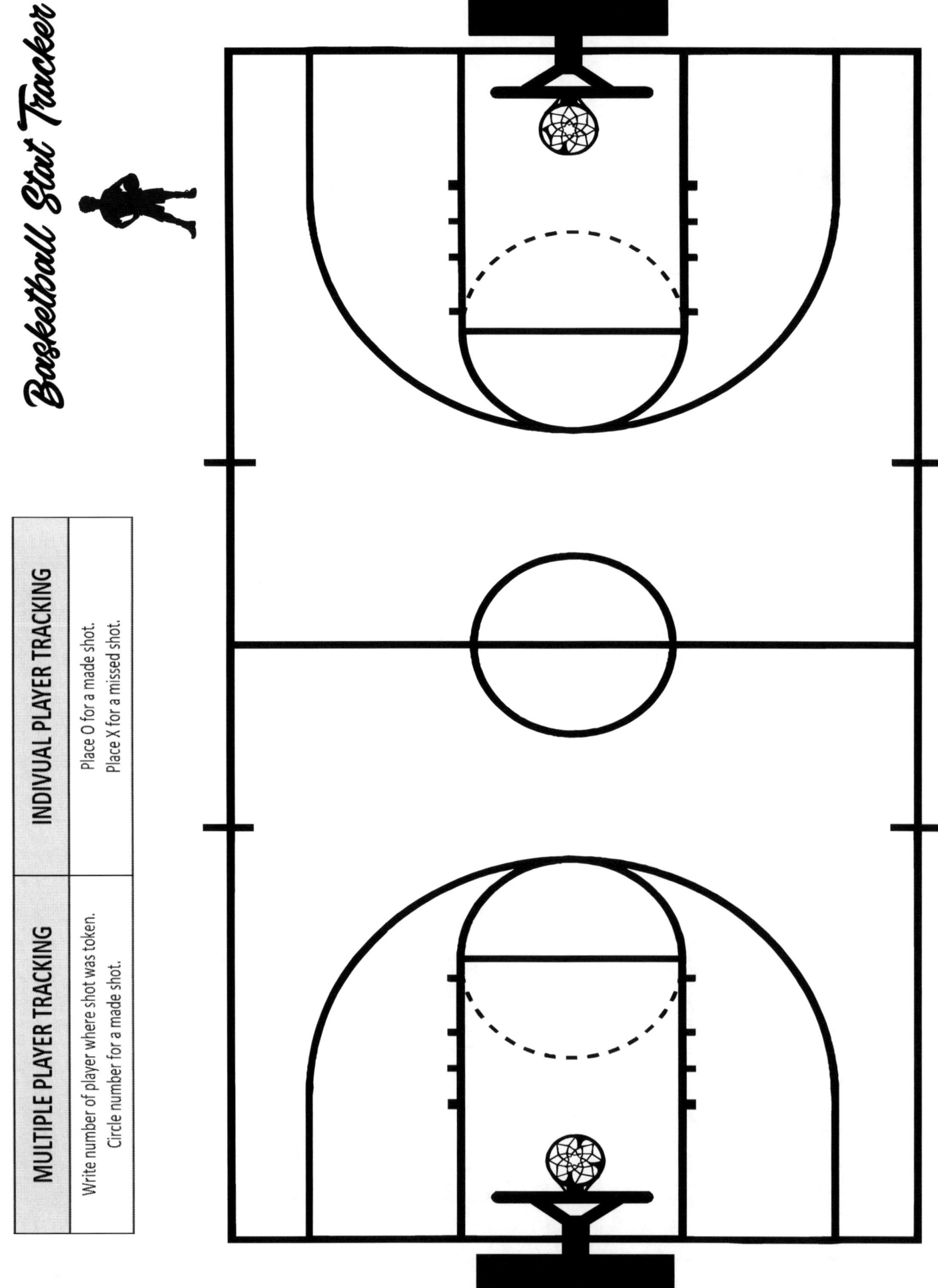

Basketball Stat Tracker

VISITORS	
HOME	
LOCATION	

SCORE	
HALF	
FINAL	

DATE

#	PLAYER	FLS					2-POINT FG		3-POINT FG		FREE THROW		REBOUND		AST	TO	STL	BLK	TOTAL POINTS
							ATT	MADE	ATT	MADE	ATT	MADE	OFF	DEF					
		1	2	3	1														
		4	5		2														
		1	2	3	1														
		4	5		2														
		1	2	3	1														
		4	5		2														
		1	2	3	1														
		4	5		2														
		1	2	3	1														
		4	5		2														
		1	2	3	1														
		4	5		2														
		1	2	3	1														
		4	5		2														
		1	2	3	1														
		4	5		2														
		1	2	3	1														
		4	5		2														
		1	2	3	1														
		4	5		2														
		1	2	3	1														
		4	5		2														
		1	2	3	1														
		4	5		2														
		1	2	3	1														
		4	5		2														
		1	2	3	1														
		4	5		2														
TEAM TOTALS																			

Basketball Stat Tracker

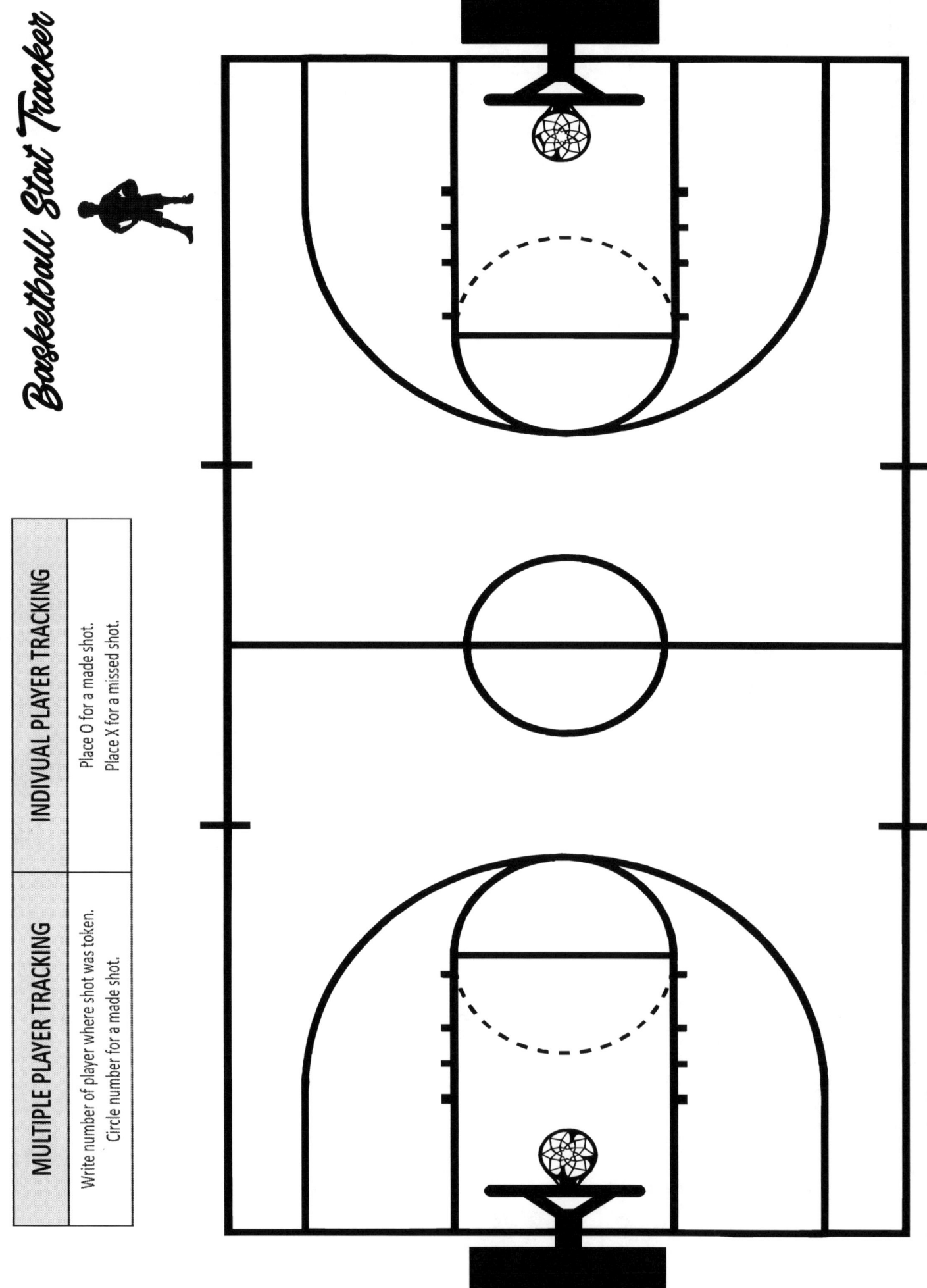

MULTIPLE PLAYER TRACKING	INDIVUAL PLAYER TRACKING
Write number of player where shot was token. Circle number for a made shot.	Place O for a made shot. Place X for a missed shot.

Basketball Stat Tracker

VISITORS	
HOME	
LOCATION	

SCORE	
HALF	
FINAL	

DATE

#	PLAYER	FLS	2-POINT FG		3-POINT FG		FREE THROW		REBOUND		AST	TO	STL	BLK	TOTAL POINTS
			ATT	MADE	ATT	MADE	ATT	MADE	OFF	DEF					
		1 2 3 4 5 1 2													
		1 2 3 4 5 1 2													
		1 2 3 4 5 1 2													
		1 2 3 4 5 1 2													
		1 2 3 4 5 1 2													
		1 2 3 4 5 1 2													
		1 2 3 4 5 1 2													
		1 2 3 4 5 1 2													
		1 2 3 4 5 1 2													
		1 2 3 4 5 1 2													
		1 2 3 4 5 1 2													
		1 2 3 4 5 1 2													
		1 2 3 4 5 1 2													
	TEAM TOTALS														

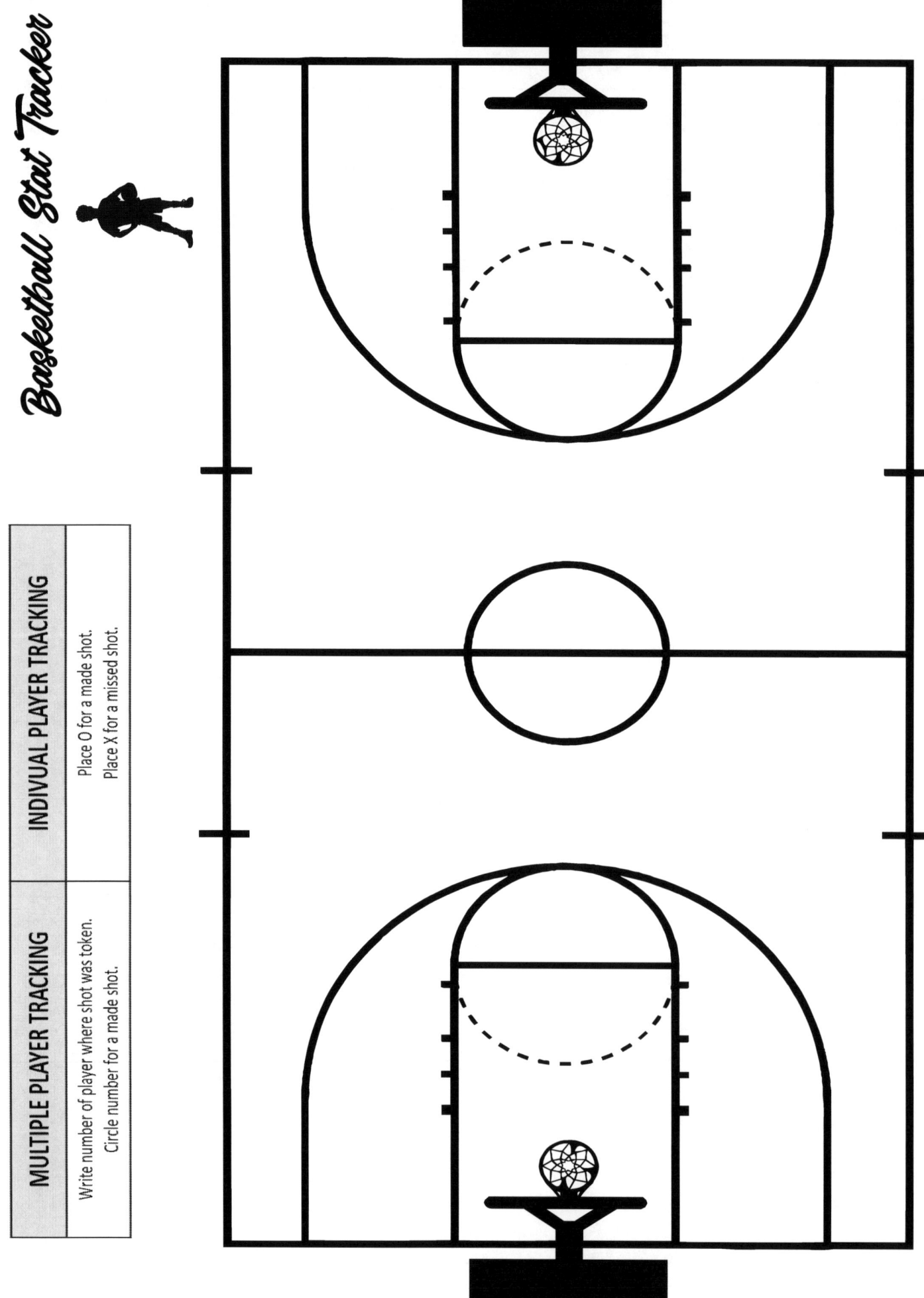

Basketball Stat Tracker

MULTIPLE PLAYER TRACKING

Write number of player where shot was token.
Circle number for a made shot.

INDIVIUAL PLAYER TRACKING

Place O for a made shot.
Place X for a missed shot.

Basketball Stat Tracker

VISITORS	
HOME	
LOCATION	

SCORE	
HALF	
FINAL	

DATE

#	PLAYER	FLS	2-POINT FG		3-POINT FG		FREE THROW		REBOUND		AST	TO	STL	BLK	TOTAL POINTS
			ATT	MADE	ATT	MADE	ATT	MADE	OFF	DEF					
		1 2 3 4 5 1 2													
		1 2 3 4 5 1 2													
		1 2 3 4 5 1 2													
		1 2 3 4 5 1 2													
		1 2 3 4 5 1 2													
		1 2 3 4 5 1 2													
		1 2 3 4 5 1 2													
		1 2 3 4 5 1 2													
		1 2 3 4 5 1 2													
		1 2 3 4 5 1 2													
		1 2 3 4 5 1 2													
		1 2 3 4 5 1 2													
		1 2 3 4 5 1 2													
		1 2 3 4 5 1 2													
	TEAM TOTALS														

Basketball Stat Tracker

MULTIPLE PLAYER TRACKING	INDIVUAL PLAYER TRACKING
Write number of player where shot was token. Circle number for a made shot.	Place O for a made shot. Place X for a missed shot.

Basketball Stat Tracker

VISITORS	
HOME	
LOCATION	

SCORE	
HALF	
FINAL	

DATE

#	PLAYER	FLS		2-POINT FG		3-POINT FG		FREE THROW		REBOUND		AST	TO	STL	BLK	TOTAL POINTS
				ATT	MADE	ATT	MADE	ATT	MADE	OFF	DEF					
		1 2 3 4 5 1 2														
		1 2 3 4 5 1 2														
		1 2 3 4 5 1 2														
		1 2 3 4 5 1 2														
		1 2 3 4 5 1 2														
		1 2 3 4 5 1 2														
		1 2 3 4 5 1 2														
		1 2 3 4 5 1 2														
		1 2 3 4 5 1 2														
		1 2 3 4 5 1 2														
		1 2 3 4 5 1 2														
		1 2 3 4 5 1 2														
		1 2 3 4 5 1 2														
TEAM TOTALS																

Basketball Stat Tracker

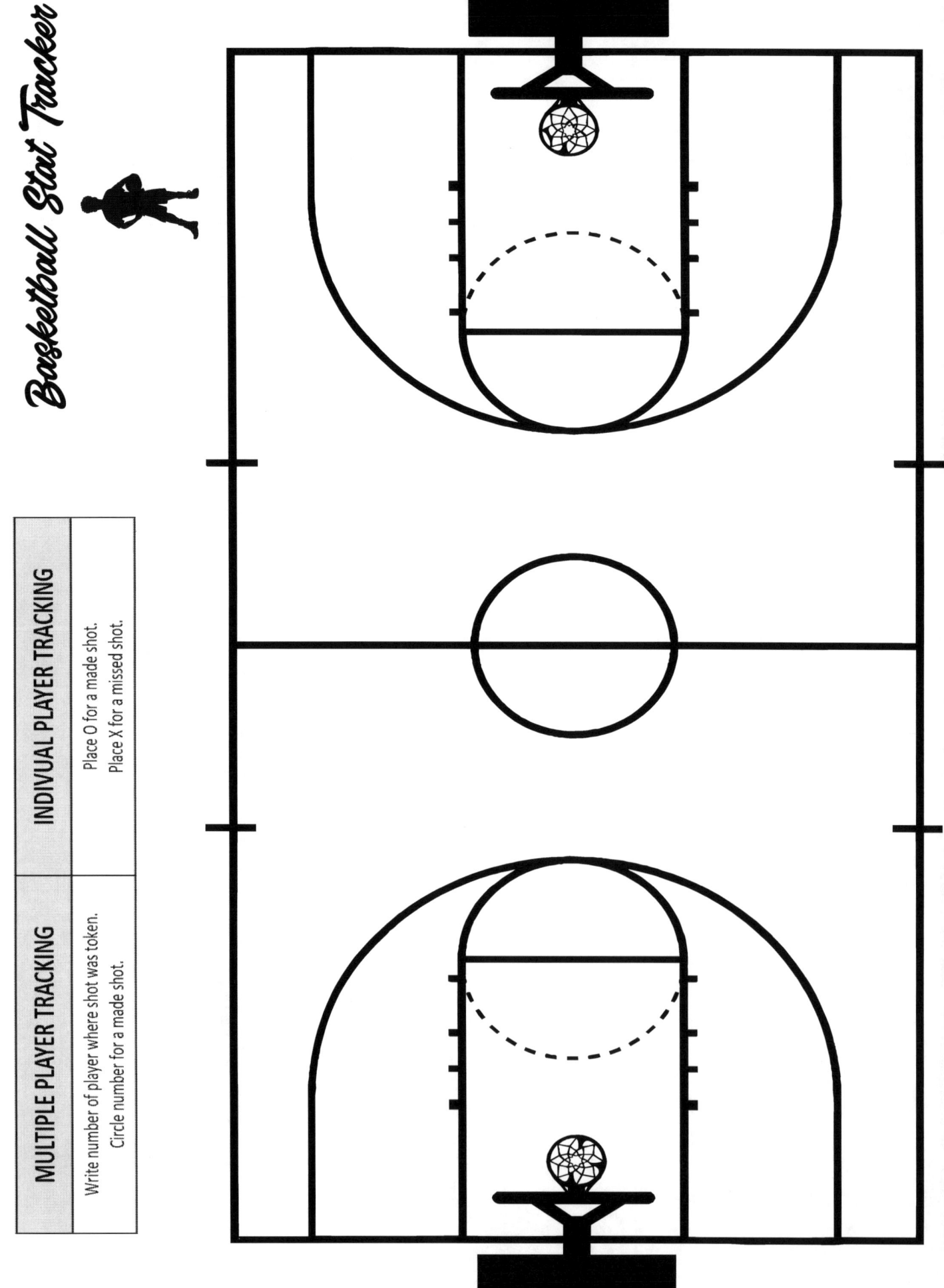

MULTIPLE PLAYER TRACKING	INDIVUAL PLAYER TRACKING
Write number of player where shot was token. Circle number for a made shot.	Place O for a made shot. Place X for a missed shot.

Basketball Stat Tracker

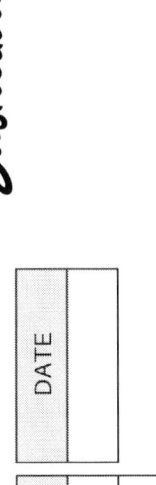

VISITORS	
HOME	
LOCATION	

SCORE	
HALF	
FINAL	

DATE

#	PLAYER	FLS		2-POINT FG		3-POINT FG		FREE THROW		REBOUND		AST	TO	STL	BLK	TOTAL POINTS
				ATT	MADE	ATT	MADE	ATT	MADE	OFF	DEF					
		1 2 3 / 1	4 5 / 2													
		1 2 3 / 1	4 5 / 2													
		1 2 3 / 1	4 5 / 2													
		1 2 3 / 1	4 5 / 2													
		1 2 3 / 1	4 5 / 2													
		1 2 3 / 1	4 5 / 2													
		1 2 3 / 1	4 5 / 2													
		1 2 3 / 1	4 5 / 2													
		1 2 3 / 1	4 5 / 2													
		1 2 3 / 1	4 5 / 2													
		1 2 3 / 1	4 5 / 2													
		1 2 3 / 1	4 5 / 2													
		1 2 3 / 1	4 5 / 2													
		1 2 3 / 1	4 5 / 2													
		1 2 3 / 1	4 5 / 2													
	TEAM TOTALS															

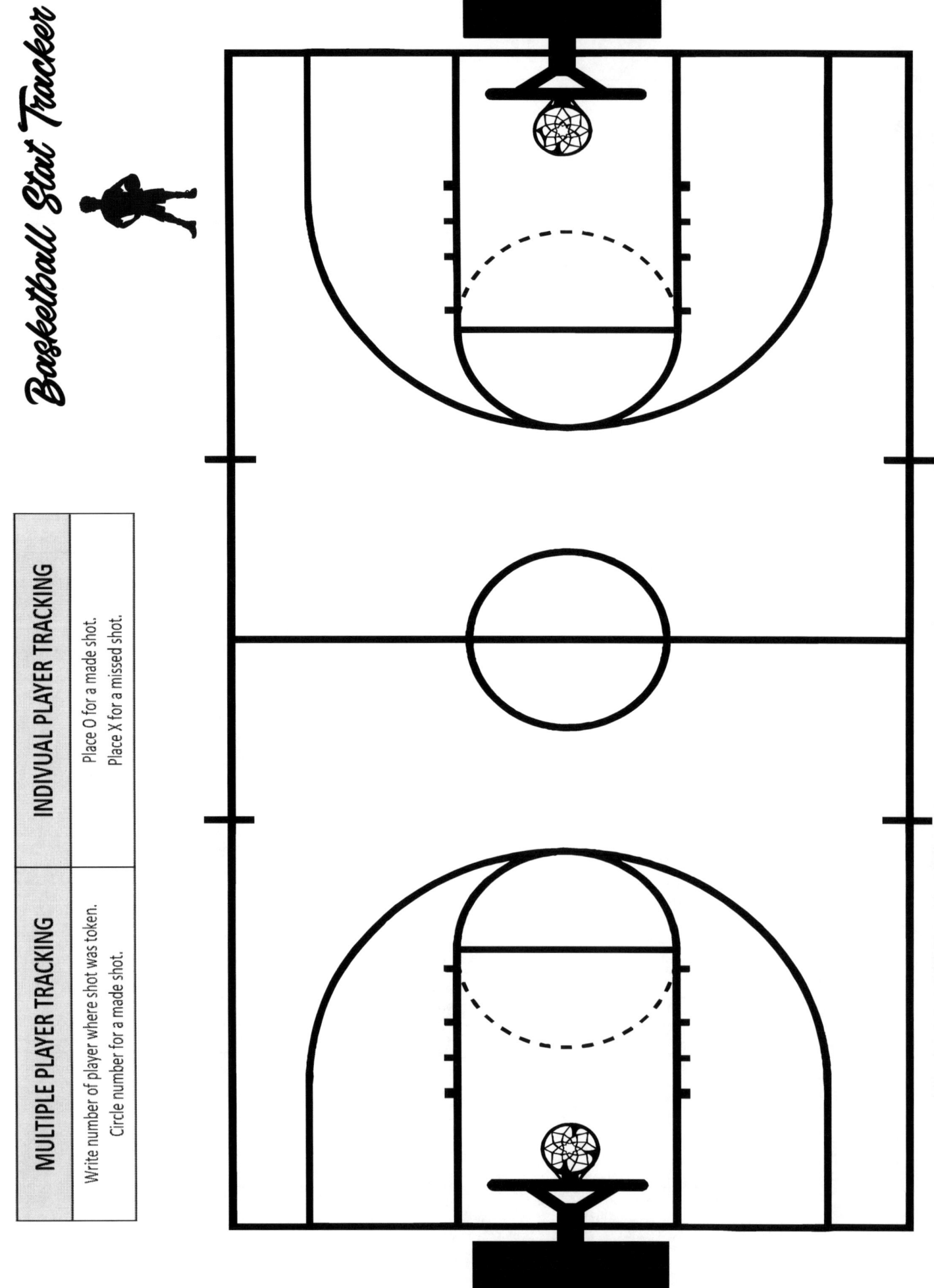

Basketball Stat Tracker

MULTIPLE PLAYER TRACKING	INDIVUAL PLAYER TRACKING
Write number of player where shot was token. Circle number for a made shot.	Place O for a made shot. Place X for a missed shot.

Basketball Stat Tracker

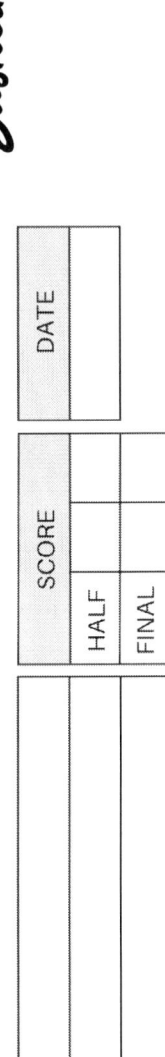

VISITORS	
HOME	
LOCATION	

SCORE		
HALF		
FINAL		

DATE

#	PLAYER	FLS		2-POINT FG		3-POINT FG		FREE THROW		REBOUND		AST	TO	STL	BLK	TOTAL POINTS
				ATT	MADE	ATT	MADE	ATT	MADE	OFF	DEF					
		1 2 3 4 5	1 2													
		1 2 3 4 5	1 2													
		1 2 3 4 5	1 2													
		1 2 3 4 5	1 2													
		1 2 3 4 5	1 2													
		1 2 3 4 5	1 2													
		1 2 3 4 5	1 2													
		1 2 3 4 5	1 2													
		1 2 3 4 5	1 2													
		1 2 3 4 5	1 2													
		1 2 3 4 5	1 2													
		1 2 3 4 5	1 2													
		1 2 3 4 5	1 2													
		1 2 3 4 5	1 2													
		1 2 3 4 5	1 2													
TEAM TOTALS																

Basketball Stat Tracker

MULTIPLE PLAYER TRACKING	INDIVIDUAL PLAYER TRACKING
Write number of player where shot was token. Circle number for a made shot.	Place O for a made shot. Place X for a missed shot.

Basketball Stat Tracker

VISITORS	
HOME	
LOCATION	

SCORE	
HALF	
FINAL	

DATE

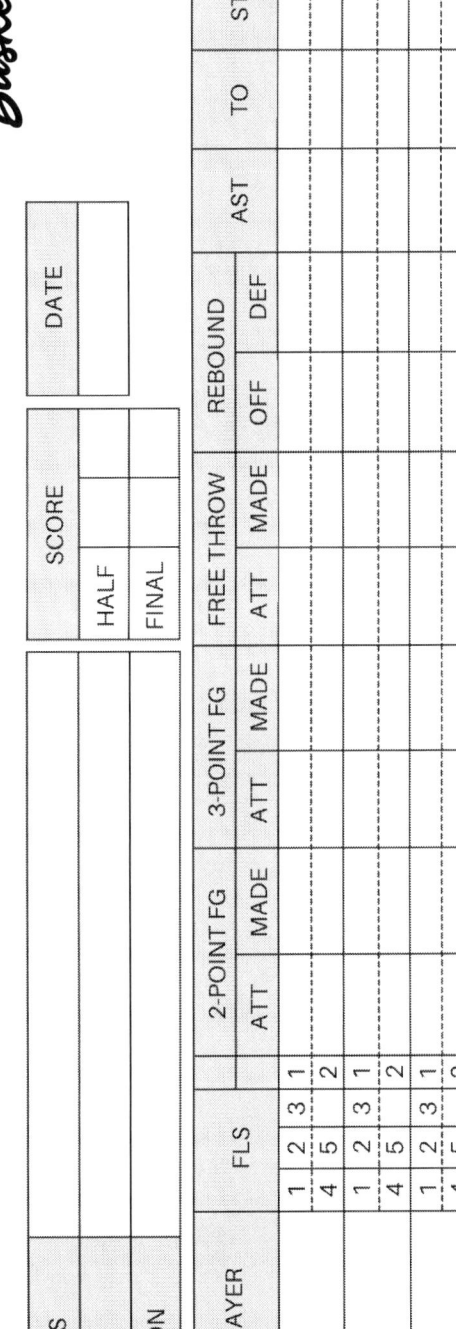

#	PLAYER	FLS	2-POINT FG		3-POINT FG		FREE THROW		REBOUND		AST	TO	STL	BLK	TOTAL POINTS
			ATT	MADE	ATT	MADE	ATT	MADE	OFF	DEF					
		1 2 3 / 4 5 / 1 2													
		1 2 3 / 4 5 / 1 2													
		1 2 3 / 4 5 / 1 2													
		1 2 3 / 4 5 / 1 2													
		1 2 3 / 4 5 / 1 2													
		1 2 3 / 4 5 / 1 2													
		1 2 3 / 4 5 / 1 2													
		1 2 3 / 4 5 / 1 2													
		1 2 3 / 4 5 / 1 2													
		1 2 3 / 4 5 / 1 2													
		1 2 3 / 4 5 / 1 2													
		1 2 3 / 4 5 / 1 2													
		1 2 3 / 4 5 / 1 2													
TEAM TOTALS															

Basketball Stat Tracker

MULTIPLE PLAYER TRACKING	INDIVUAL PLAYER TRACKING
Write number of player where shot was token. Circle number for a made shot.	Place O for a made shot. Place X for a missed shot.

Basketball Stat Tracker

VISITORS	
HOME	
LOCATION	

SCORE	
HALF	
FINAL	

DATE

#	PLAYER	FLS		2-POINT FG		3-POINT FG		FREE THROW		REBOUND		AST	TO	STL	BLK	TOTAL POINTS
				ATT	MADE	ATT	MADE	ATT	MADE	OFF	DEF					
		1 2 3 4 5	1 2													
		1 2 3 4 5	1 2													
		1 2 3 4 5	1 2													
		1 2 3 4 5	1 2													
		1 2 3 4 5	1 2													
		1 2 3 4 5	1 2													
		1 2 3 4 5	1 2													
		1 2 3 4 5	1 2													
		1 2 3 4 5	1 2													
		1 2 3 4 5	1 2													
		1 2 3 4 5	1 2													
		1 2 3 4 5	1 2													
		1 2 3 4 5	1 2													
		1 2 3 4 5	1 2													
	TEAM TOTALS															

Basketball Stat Tracker

MULTIPLE PLAYER TRACKING

Write number of player where shot was token.

Circle number for a made shot.

INDIVUAL PLAYER TRACKING

Place O for a made shot.

Place X for a missed shot.

Basketball Stat Tracker

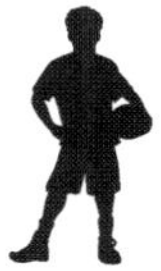

VISITORS	
HOME	
LOCATION	

SCORE		
HALF		
FINAL		

DATE

#	PLAYER	FLS		2-POINT FG		3-POINT FG		FREE THROW		REBOUND		AST	TO	STL	BLK	TOTAL POINTS
				ATT	MADE	ATT	MADE	ATT	MADE	OFF	DEF					
		1 2 3 4 5	1 2													
		1 2 3 4 5	1 2													
		1 2 3 4 5	1 2													
		1 2 3 4 5	1 2													
		1 2 3 4 5	1 2													
		1 2 3 4 5	1 2													
		1 2 3 4 5	1 2													
		1 2 3 4 5	1 2													
		1 2 3 4 5	1 2													
		1 2 3 4 5	1 2													
		1 2 3 4 5	1 2													
		1 2 3 4 5	1 2													
		1 2 3 4 5	1 2													
		1 2 3 4 5	1 2													
		1 2 3 4 5	1 2													
TEAM TOTALS																

Basketball Stat Tracker

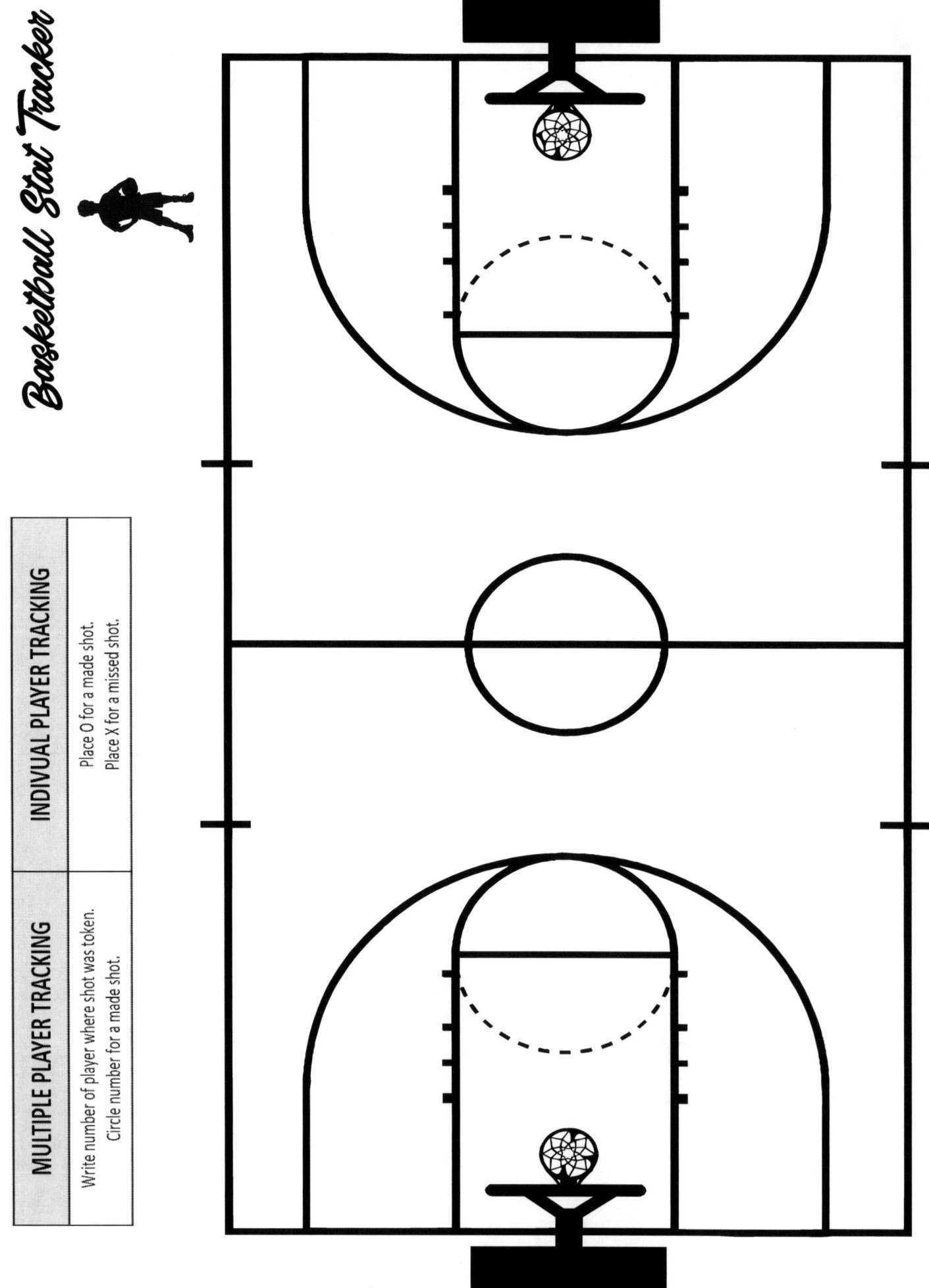

MULTIPLE PLAYER TRACKING	INDIVUAL PLAYER TRACKING
Write number of player where shot was token. Circle number for a made shot.	Place O for a made shot. Place X for a missed shot.

Basketball Stat Tracker

VISITORS	
HOME	
LOCATION	

SCORE	
HALF	
FINAL	

DATE	

#	PLAYER	FLS	2-POINT FG		3-POINT FG		FREE THROW		REBOUND		AST	TO	STL	BLK	TOTAL POINTS
			ATT	MADE	ATT	MADE	ATT	MADE	OFF	DEF					
		1 2 3 4 5 1 2													
		1 2 3 4 5 1 2													
		1 2 3 4 5 1 2													
		1 2 3 4 5 1 2													
		1 2 3 4 5 1 2													
		1 2 3 4 5 1 2													
		1 2 3 4 5 1 2													
		1 2 3 4 5 1 2													
		1 2 3 4 5 1 2													
		1 2 3 4 5 1 2													
		1 2 3 4 5 1 2													
		1 2 3 4 5 1 2													
		1 2 3 4 5 1 2													
		1 2 3 4 5 1 2													
	TEAM TOTALS														

Basketball Stat Tracker

MULTIPLE PLAYER TRACKING	INDIVIDUAL PLAYER TRACKING
Write number of player where shot was token. Circle number for a made shot.	Place O for a made shot. Place X for a missed shot.

Basketball Stat Tracker

VISITORS	
HOME	
LOCATION	

SCORE	
HALF	
FINAL	

DATE	

#	PLAYER	FLS						2-POINT FG		3-POINT FG		FREE THROW		REBOUND		AST	TO	STL	BLK	TOTAL POINTS
								ATT	MADE	ATT	MADE	ATT	MADE	OFF	DEF					
		1	2	3			1													
		4	5				2													
		1	2	3			1													
		4	5				2													
		1	2	3			1													
		4	5				2													
		1	2	3			1													
		4	5				2													
		1	2	3			1													
		4	5				2													
		1	2	3			1													
		4	5				2													
		1	2	3			1													
		4	5				2													
		1	2	3			1													
		4	5				2													
		1	2	3			1													
		4	5				2													
		1	2	3			1													
		4	5				2													
		1	2	3			1													
		4	5				2													
		1	2	3			1													
		4	5				2													
		1	2	3			1													
		4	5				2													
		1	2	3			1													
		4	5				2													
	TEAM TOTALS																			

Basketball Stat Tracker

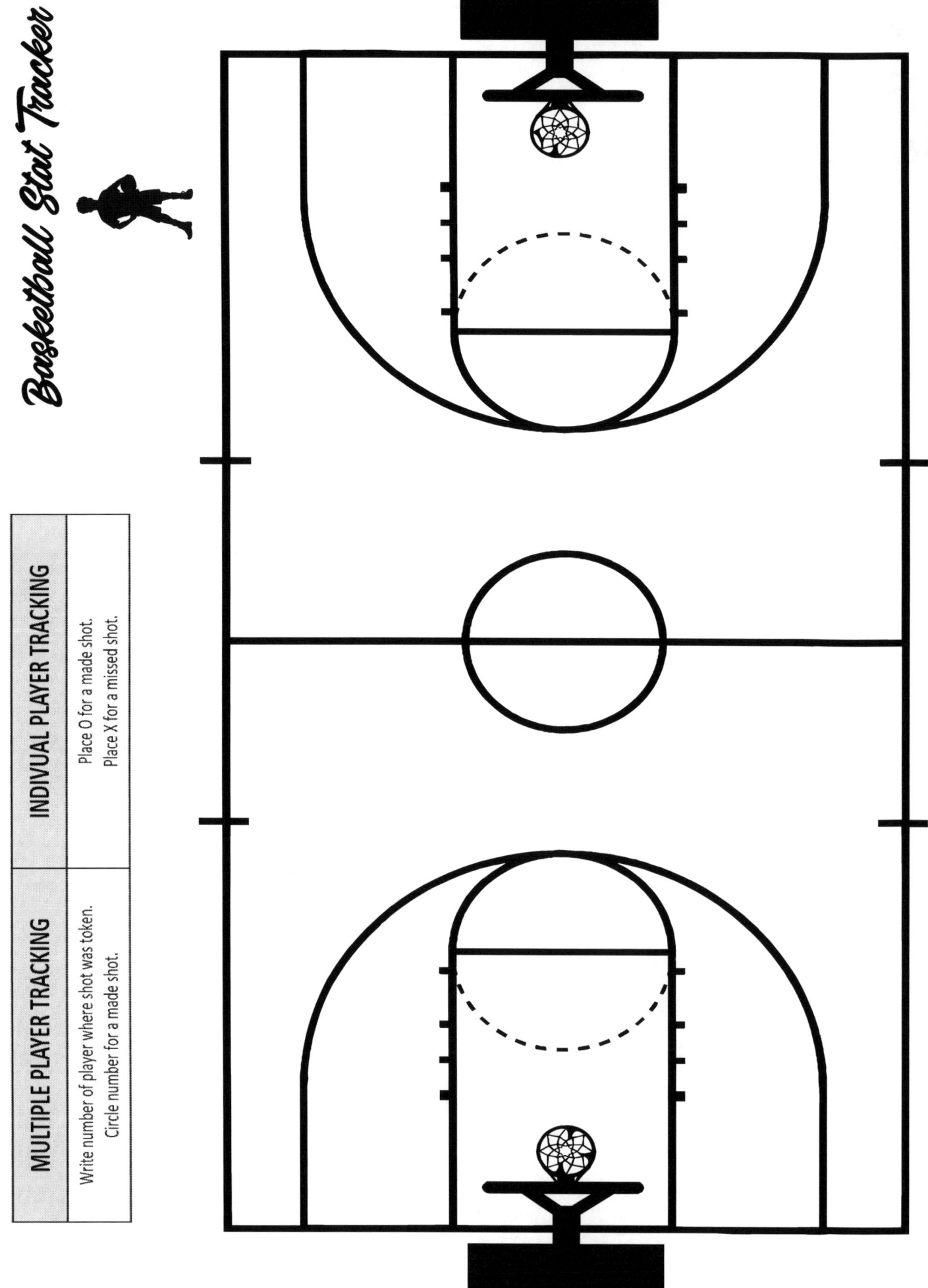

MULTIPLE PLAYER TRACKING	INDIVIDUAL PLAYER TRACKING
Write number of player where shot was token. Circle number for a made shot.	Place O for a made shot. Place X for a missed shot.

Basketball Stat Tracker

VISITORS	
HOME	
LOCATION	

SCORE	
HALF	
FINAL	

DATE

#	PLAYER	FLS		2-POINT FG		3-POINT FG		FREE THROW		REBOUND		AST	TO	STL	BLK	TOTAL POINTS
				ATT	MADE	ATT	MADE	ATT	MADE	OFF	DEF					
		1 2 3 4 5	1 2													
		1 2 3 4 5	1 2													
		1 2 3 4 5	1 2													
		1 2 3 4 5	1 2													
		1 2 3 4 5	1 2													
		1 2 3 4 5	1 2													
		1 2 3 4 5	1 2													
		1 2 3 4 5	1 2													
		1 2 3 4 5	1 2													
		1 2 3 4 5	1 2													
		1 2 3 4 5	1 2													
		1 2 3 4 5	1 2													
		1 2 3 4 5	1 2													
		1 2 3 4 5	1 2													
	TEAM TOTALS															

Basketball Stat Tracker

MULTIPLE PLAYER TRACKING	INDIVUAL PLAYER TRACKING
Write number of player where shot was token. Circle number for a made shot.	Place O for a made shot. Place X for a missed shot.

Basketball Stat Tracker

VISITORS	
HOME	
LOCATION	

SCORE	
HALF	
FINAL	

DATE	

#	PLAYER	FLS			2-POINT FG		3-POINT FG		FREE THROW		REBOUND		AST	TO	STL	BLK	TOTAL POINTS
					ATT	MADE	ATT	MADE	ATT	MADE	OFF	DEF					
		1 2 3 4 5	1 2														
		1 2 3 4 5	1 2														
		1 2 3 4 5	1 2														
		1 2 3 4 5	1 2														
		1 2 3 4 5	1 2														
		1 2 3 4 5	1 2														
		1 2 3 4 5	1 2														
		1 2 3 4 5	1 2														
		1 2 3 4 5	1 2														
		1 2 3 4 5	1 2														
		1 2 3 4 5	1 2														
		1 2 3 4 5	1 2														
		1 2 3 4 5	1 2														
	TEAM TOTALS																

Basketball Stat Tracker

MULTIPLE PLAYER TRACKING	INDIVUAL PLAYER TRACKING
Write number of player where shot was token. Circle number for a made shot.	Place O for a made shot. Place X for a missed shot.

Basketball Stat Tracker

VISITORS	
HOME	
LOCATION	

SCORE	
HALF	
FINAL	

DATE

#	PLAYER	FLS		2-POINT FG.		3-POINT FG		FREE THROW		REBOUND		AST	TO	STL	BLK	TOTAL POINTS
				ATT	MADE	ATT	MADE	ATT	MADE	OFF	DEF					
		1 2 3 1 4 5 2														
		1 2 3 1 4 5 2														
		1 2 3 1 4 5 2														
		1 2 3 1 4 5 2														
		1 2 3 1 4 5 2														
		1 2 3 1 4 5 2														
		1 2 3 1 4 5 2														
		1 2 3 1 4 5 2														
		1 2 3 1 4 5 2														
		1 2 3 1 4 5 2														
		1 2 3 1 4 5 2														
		1 2 3 1 4 5 2														
		1 2 3 1 4 5 2														
		1 2 3 1 4 5 2														
	TEAM TOTALS															

Basketball Stat Tracker

MULTIPLE PLAYER TRACKING	INDIVIDUAL PLAYER TRACKING
Write number of player where shot was token. Circle number for a made shot.	Place O for a made shot. Place X for a missed shot.

Basketball Stat Tracker

VISITORS	
HOME	
LOCATION	

SCORE	
HALF	
FINAL	

DATE	

#	PLAYER	FLS		2-POINT FG		3-POINT FG		FREE THROW		REBOUND		AST	TO	STL	BLK	TOTAL POINTS
				ATT	MADE	ATT	MADE	ATT	MADE	OFF	DEF					
		1 2 3 / 4 5 1 2														
		1 2 3 / 4 5 1 2														
		1 2 3 / 4 5 1 2														
		1 2 3 / 4 5 1 2														
		1 2 3 / 4 5 1 2														
		1 2 3 / 4 5 1 2														
		1 2 3 / 4 5 1 2														
		1 2 3 / 4 5 1 2														
		1 2 3 / 4 5 1 2														
		1 2 3 / 4 5 1 2														
		1 2 3 / 4 5 1 2														
		1 2 3 / 4 5 1 2														
		1 2 3 / 4 5 1 2														
		1 2 3 / 4 5 1 2														
TEAM TOTALS																

Basketball Stat Tracker

MULTIPLE PLAYER TRACKING	INDIVUAL PLAYER TRACKING
Write number of player where shot was token.	Place O for a made shot.
Circle number for a made shot.	Place X for a missed shot.

Basketball Stat Tracker

VISITORS	
HOME	
LOCATION	

SCORE	
HALF	
FINAL	

DATE

#	PLAYER	FLS		2-POINT FG		3-POINT FG		FREE THROW		REBOUND		AST	TO	STL	BLK	TOTAL POINTS
				ATT	MADE	ATT	MADE	ATT	MADE	OFF	DEF					
		1 2 3 4 5	1 2													
		1 2 3 4 5	1 2													
		1 2 3 4 5	1 2													
		1 2 3 4 5	1 2													
		1 2 3 4 5	1 2													
		1 2 3 4 5	1 2													
		1 2 3 4 5	1 2													
		1 2 3 4 5	1 2													
		1 2 3 4 5	1 2													
		1 2 3 4 5	1 2													
		1 2 3 4 5	1 2													
		1 2 3 4 5	1 2													
		1 2 3 4 5	1 2													
		1 2 3 4 5	1 2													
	TEAM TOTALS															

Basketball Stat Tracker

MULTIPLE PLAYER TRACKING

Write number of player where shot was token.

Circle number for a made shot.

INDIVUAL PLAYER TRACKING

Place O for a made shot.

Place X for a missed shot.

Basketball Stat Tracker

VISITORS	
HOME	
LOCATION	

SCORE	
HALF	
FINAL	

DATE

#	PLAYER	FLS	2-POINT FG		3-POINT FG		FREE THROW		REBOUND		AST	TO	STL	BLK	TOTAL POINTS
			ATT	MADE	ATT	MADE	ATT	MADE	OFF	DEF					
		1 2 3 / 1 4 5 / 2													
		1 2 3 / 1 4 5 / 2													
		1 2 3 / 1 4 5 / 2													
		1 2 3 / 1 4 5 / 2													
		1 2 3 / 1 4 5 / 2													
		1 2 3 / 1 4 5 / 2													
		1 2 3 / 1 4 5 / 2													
		1 2 3 / 1 4 5 / 2													
		1 2 3 / 1 4 5 / 2													
		1 2 3 / 1 4 5 / 2													
		1 2 3 / 1 4 5 / 2													
		1 2 3 / 1 4 5 / 2													
		1 2 3 / 1 4 5 / 2													
		1 2 3 / 1 4 5 / 2													
		1 2 3 / 1 4 5 / 2													
	TEAM TOTALS														

Basketball Stat Tracker

MULTIPLE PLAYER TRACKING	INDIVUAL PLAYER TRACKING
Write number of player where shot was token.	Place O for a made shot.
Circle number for a made shot.	Place X for a missed shot.

Basketball Stat Tracker

VISITORS	
HOME	
LOCATION	

SCORE	
HALF	
FINAL	

DATE

#	PLAYER	FLS			2-POINT FG		3-POINT FG		FREE THROW		REBOUND		AST	TO	STL	BLK	TOTAL POINTS
					ATT	MADE	ATT	MADE	ATT	MADE	OFF	DEF					
		1 2 3	1														
		4 5	2														
		1 2 3	1														
		4 5	2														
		1 2 3	1														
		4 5	2														
		1 2 3	1														
		4 5	2														
		1 2 3	1														
		4 5	2														
		1 2 3	1														
		4 5	2														
		1 2 3	1														
		4 5	2														
		1 2 3	1														
		4 5	2														
		1 2 3	1														
		4 5	2														
		1 2 3	1														
		4 5	2														
		1 2 3	1														
		4 5	2														
		1 2 3	1														
		4 5	2														
		1 2 3	1														
		4 5	2														
		1 2 3	1														
		4 5	2														
TEAM TOTALS																	

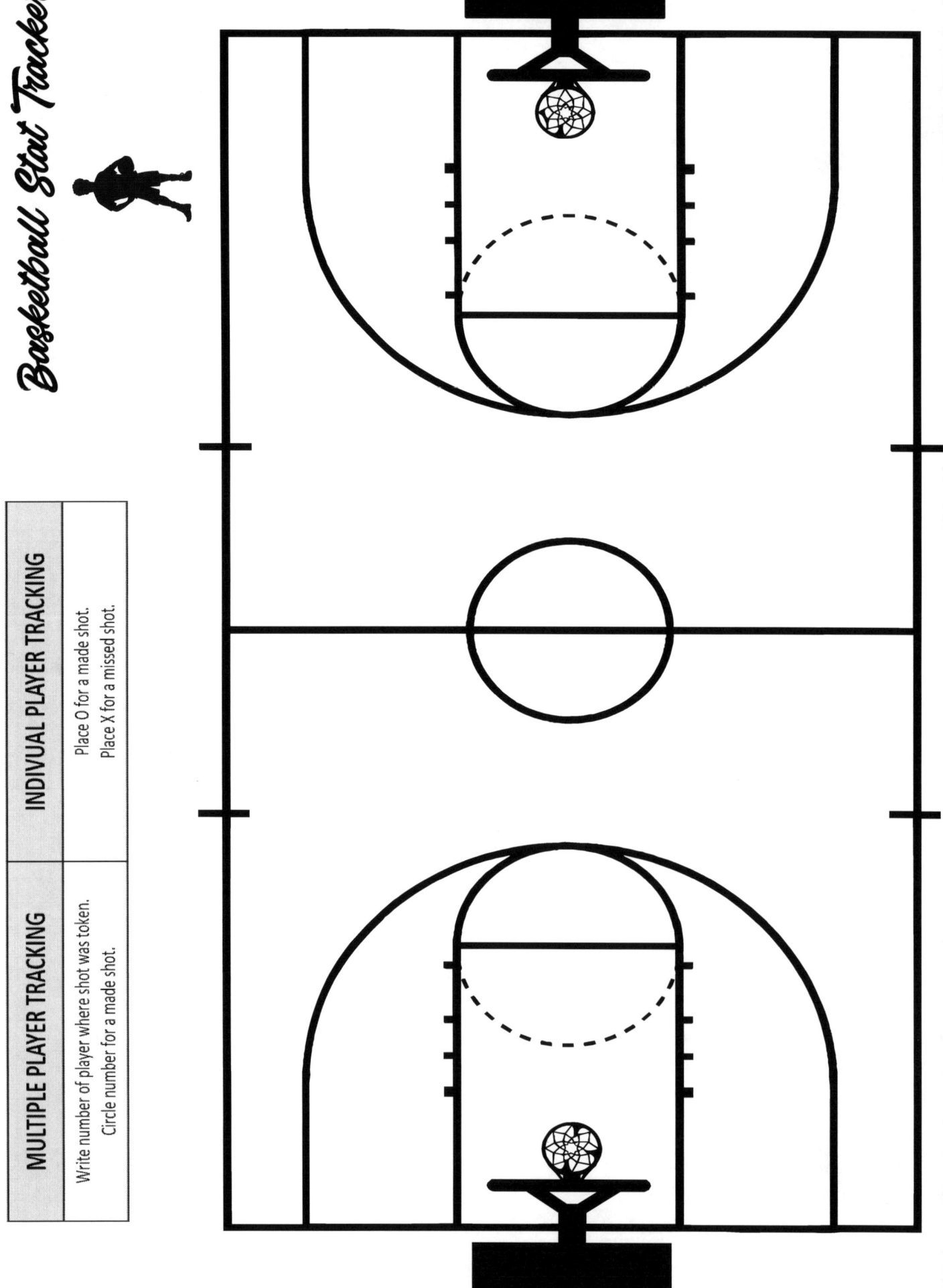

Basketball Stat Tracker

MULTIPLE PLAYER TRACKING	INDIVUAL PLAYER TRACKING
Write number of player where shot was token. Circle number for a made shot.	Place O for a made shot. Place X for a missed shot.

Basketball Stat Tracker

VISITORS	
HOME	
LOCATION	

SCORE	
HALF	
FINAL	

DATE	

#	PLAYER	FLS	2-POINT FG ATT	2-POINT FG MADE	3-POINT FG ATT	3-POINT FG MADE	FREE THROW ATT	FREE THROW MADE	REBOUND OFF	REBOUND DEF	AST	TO	STL	BLK	TOTAL POINTS
		1 2 3 4 5 1 2													
		1 2 3 4 5 1 2													
		1 2 3 4 5 1 2													
		1 2 3 4 5 1 2													
		1 2 3 4 5 1 2													
		1 2 3 4 5 1 2													
		1 2 3 4 5 1 2													
		1 2 3 4 5 1 2													
		1 2 3 4 5 1 2													
		1 2 3 4 5 1 2													
		1 2 3 4 5 1 2													
		1 2 3 4 5 1 2													
		1 2 3 4 5 1 2													
		1 2 3 4 5 1 2													
TEAM TOTALS															

Basketball Stat Tracker

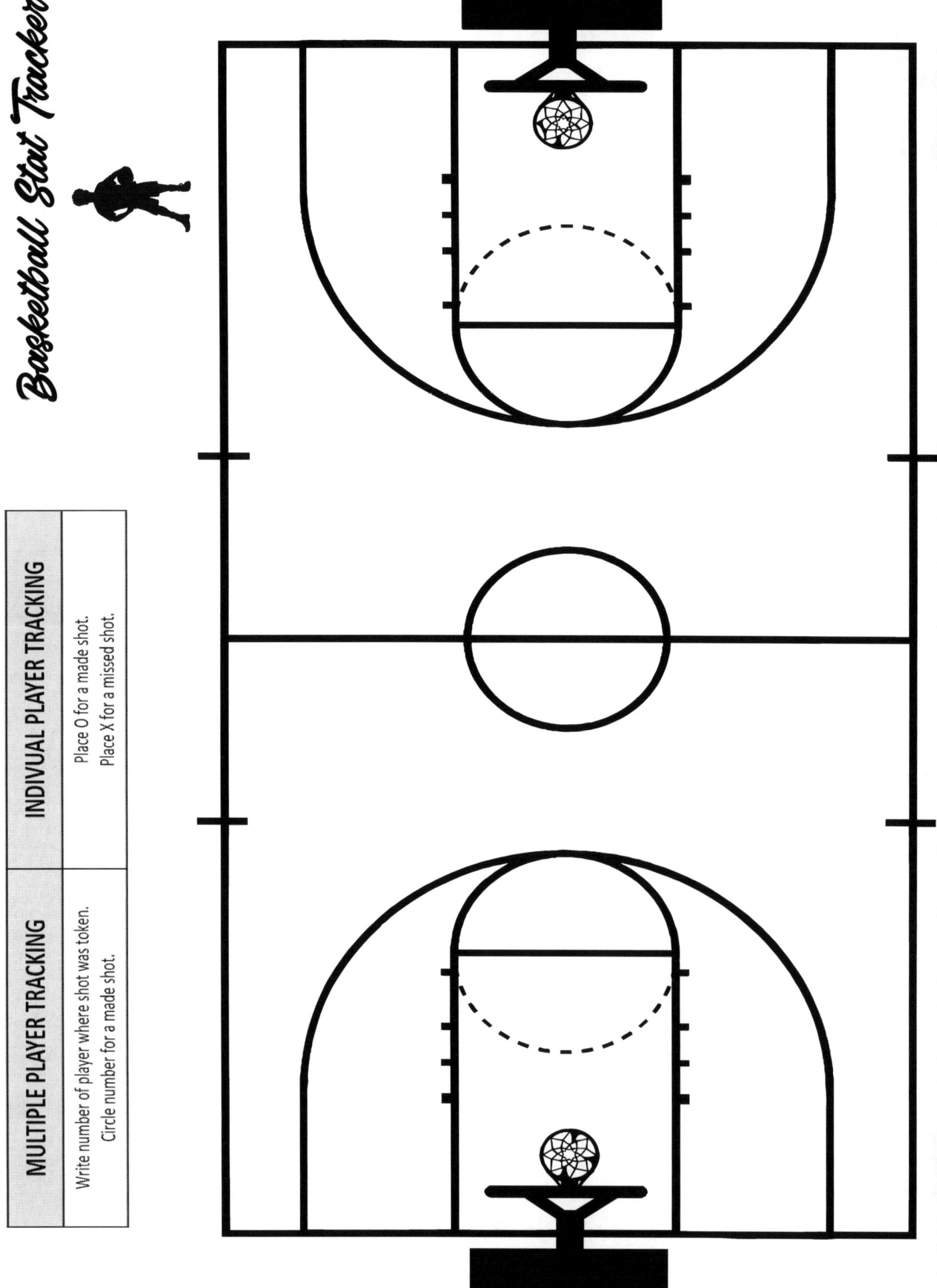

MULTIPLE PLAYER TRACKING

Write number of player where shot was token.
Circle number for a made shot.

INDIVUAL PLAYER TRACKING

Place O for a made shot.
Place X for a missed shot.

Basketball Stat Tracker

VISITORS	
HOME	
LOCATION	

SCORE	
HALF	
FINAL	

DATE

#	PLAYER	FLS		2-POINT FG		3-POINT FG		FREE THROW		REBOUND		AST	TO	STL	BLK	TOTAL POINTS
				ATT	MADE	ATT	MADE	ATT	MADE	OFF	DEF					
		1 2 3 4 5	1 2													
		1 2 3 4 5	1 2													
		1 2 3 4 5	1 2													
		1 2 3 4 5	1 2													
		1 2 3 4 5	1 2													
		1 2 3 4 5	1 2													
		1 2 3 4 5	1 2													
		1 2 3 4 5	1 2													
		1 2 3 4 5	1 2													
		1 2 3 4 5	1 2													
		1 2 3 4 5	1 2													
		1 2 3 4 5	1 2													
		1 2 3 4 5	1 2													
		1 2 3 4 5	1 2													
	TEAM TOTALS															

Basketball Stat Tracker

MULTIPLE PLAYER TRACKING	INDIVUAL PLAYER TRACKING
Write number of player where shot was token. Circle number for a made shot.	Place O for a made shot. Place X for a missed shot.

Basketball Stat Tracker

VISITORS	
HOME	
LOCATION	

SCORE	
HALF	
FINAL	

DATE	

#	PLAYER	FLS		2-POINT FG		3-POINT FG		FREE THROW		REBOUND		AST	TO	STL	BLK	TOTAL POINTS
				ATT	MADE	ATT	MADE	ATT	MADE	OFF	DEF					
		1 2 3 4 5	1 2													
		1 2 3 4 5	1 2													
		1 2 3 4 5	1 2													
		1 2 3 4 5	1 2													
		1 2 3 4 5	1 2													
		1 2 3 4 5	1 2													
		1 2 3 4 5	1 2													
		1 2 3 4 5	1 2													
		1 2 3 4 5	1 2													
		1 2 3 4 5	1 2													
		1 2 3 4 5	1 2													
		1 2 3 4 5	1 2													
		1 2 3 4 5	1 2													
		1 2 3 4 5	1 2													
TEAM TOTALS																

Basketball Stat Tracker

MULTIPLE PLAYER TRACKING

Write number of player where shot was taken.
Circle number for a made shot.

INDIVUAL PLAYER TRACKING

Place O for a made shot.
Place X for a missed shot.

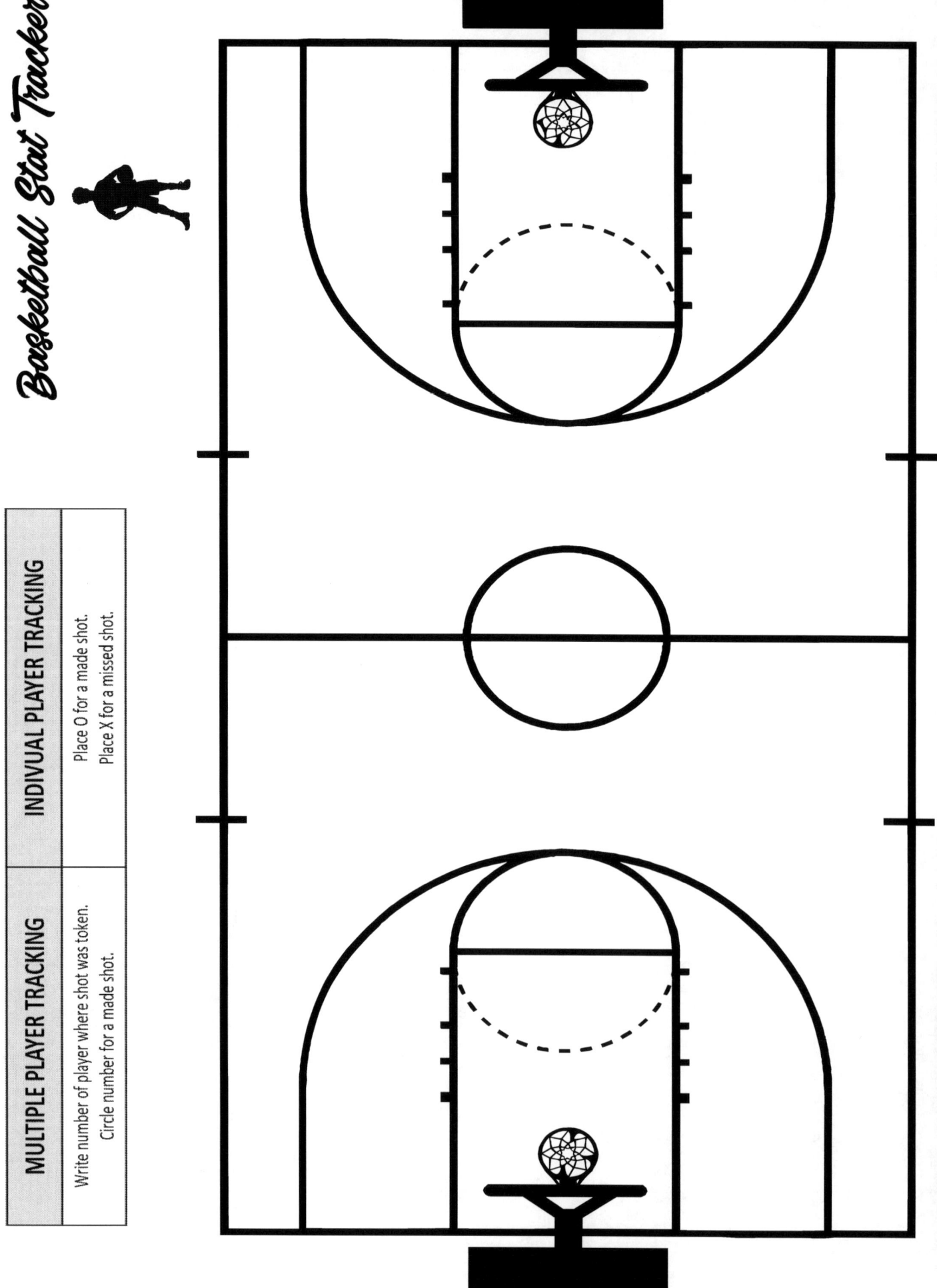

Basketball Stat Tracker

VISITORS	
HOME	
LOCATION	

SCORE	
HALF	
FINAL	

DATE

#	PLAYER	FLS	2-POINT FG		3-POINT FG		FREE THROW		REBOUND		AST	TO	STL	BLK	TOTAL POINTS
			ATT	MADE	ATT	MADE	ATT	MADE	OFF	DEF					
		1 2 3 1 / 4 5 2													
		1 2 3 1 / 4 5 2													
		1 2 3 1 / 4 5 2													
		1 2 3 1 / 4 5 2													
		1 2 3 1 / 4 5 2													
		1 2 3 1 / 4 5 2													
		1 2 3 1 / 4 5 2													
		1 2 3 1 / 4 5 2													
		1 2 3 1 / 4 5 2													
		1 2 3 1 / 4 5 2													
		1 2 3 1 / 4 5 2													
		1 2 3 1 / 4 5 2													
		1 2 3 1 / 4 5 2													
		1 2 3 1 / 4 5 2													
	TEAM TOTALS														

Basketball Stat Tracker

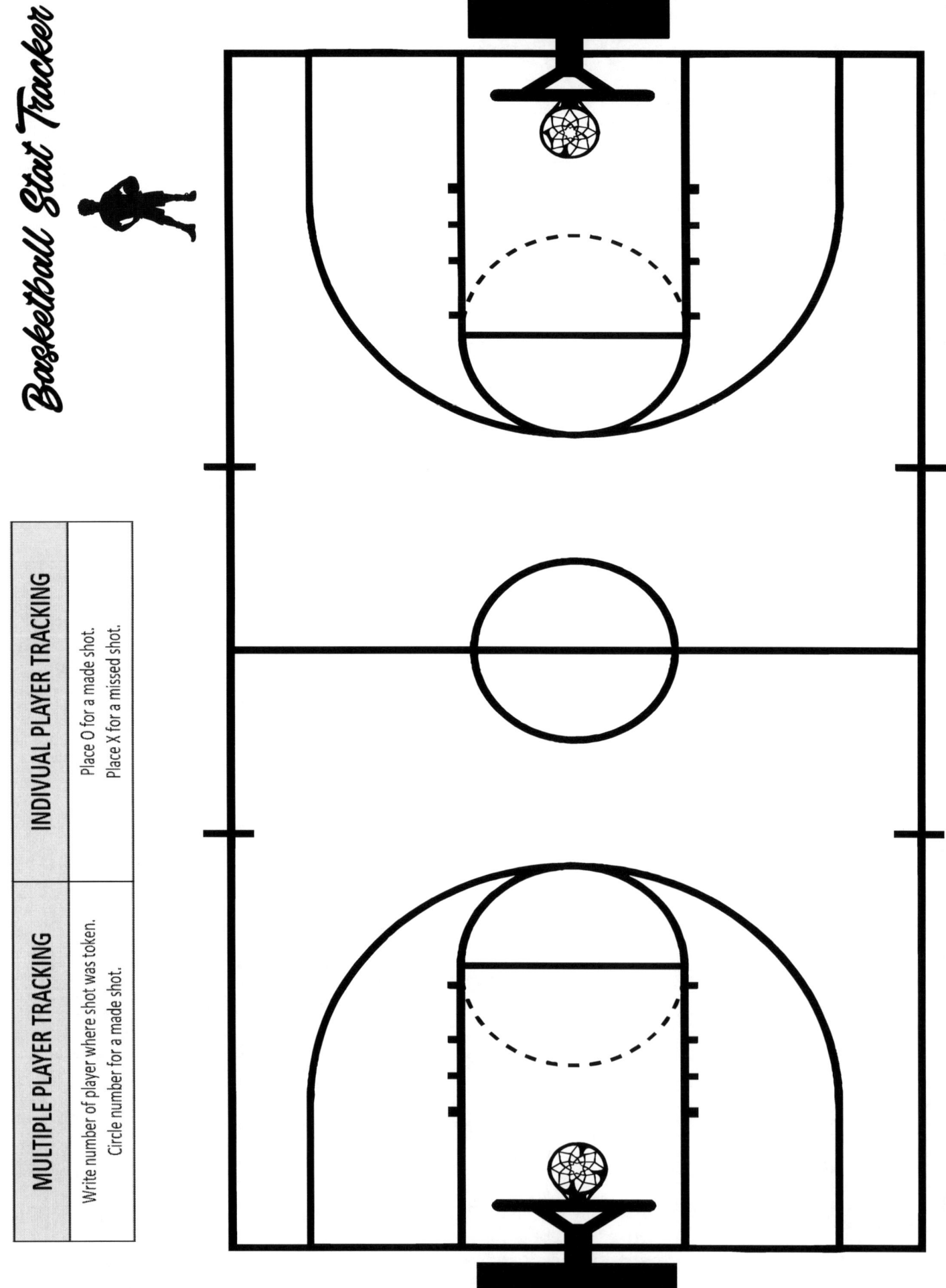

MULTIPLE PLAYER TRACKING	INDIVUAL PLAYER TRACKING
Write number of player where shot was token. Circle number for a made shot.	Place O for a made shot. Place X for a missed shot.

Basketball Stat Tracker

VISITORS	
HOME	
LOCATION	

SCORE	
HALF	
FINAL	

DATE

#	PLAYER	FLS			2-POINT FG		3-POINT FG		FREE THROW		REBOUND		AST	TO	STL	BLK	TOTAL POINTS
					ATT	MADE	ATT	MADE	ATT	MADE	OFF	DEF					
		1 2 3	1														
		4 5	2														
		1 2 3	1														
		4 5	2														
		1 2 3	1														
		4 5	2														
		1 2 3	1														
		4 5	2														
		1 2 3	1														
		4 5	2														
		1 2 3	1														
		4 5	2														
		1 2 3	1														
		4 5	2														
		1 2 3	1														
		4 5	2														
		1 2 3	1														
		4 5	2														
		1 2 3	1														
		4 5	2														
		1 2 3	1														
		4 5	2														
		1 2 3	1														
		4 5	2														
		1 2 3	1														
		4 5	2														
	TEAM TOTALS																

Basketball Stat Tracker

MULTIPLE PLAYER TRACKING	INDIVUAL PLAYER TRACKING
Write number of player where shot was token. Circle number for a made shot.	Place O for a made shot. Place X for a missed shot.

Basketball Stat Tracker

VISITORS	
HOME	
LOCATION	

SCORE	
HALF	
FINAL	

DATE

#	PLAYER	FLS		2-POINT FG		3-POINT FG		FREE THROW		REBOUND		AST	TO	STL	BLK	TOTAL POINTS
				ATT	MADE	ATT	MADE	ATT	MADE	OFF	DEF					
		1 2 3 4 5	1 2													
		1 2 3 4 5	1 2													
		1 2 3 4 5	1 2													
		1 2 3 4 5	1 2													
		1 2 3 4 5	1 2													
		1 2 3 4 5	1 2													
		1 2 3 4 5	1 2													
		1 2 3 4 5	1 2													
		1 2 3 4 5	1 2													
		1 2 3 4 5	1 2													
		1 2 3 4 5	1 2													
		1 2 3 4 5	1 2													
		1 2 3 4 5	1 2													
		1 2 3 4 5	1 2													
	TEAM TOTALS															

Basketball Stat Tracker

MULTIPLE PLAYER TRACKING

Write number of player where shot was token.

Circle number for a made shot.

INDIVUAL PLAYER TRACKING

Place O for a made shot.

Place X for a missed shot.

Basketball Stat Tracker

VISITORS	
HOME	
LOCATION	

SCORE	
HALF	
FINAL	

DATE	

#	PLAYER	FLS			2-POINT FG		3-POINT FG		FREE THROW		REBOUND		AST	TO	STL	BLK	TOTAL POINTS
					ATT	MADE	ATT	MADE	ATT	MADE	OFF	DEF					
		1 2 3 4 5	1 2														
		1 2 3 4 5	1 2														
		1 2 3 4 5	1 2														
		1 2 3 4 5	1 2														
		1 2 3 4 5	1 2														
		1 2 3 4 5	1 2														
		1 2 3 4 5	1 2														
		1 2 3 4 5	1 2														
		1 2 3 4 5	1 2														
		1 2 3 4 5	1 2														
		1 2 3 4 5	1 2														
		1 2 3 4 5	1 2														
		1 2 3 4 5	1 2														
		1 2 3 4 5	1 2														
	TEAM TOTALS																

Basketball Stat Tracker

MULTIPLE PLAYER TRACKING

Write number of player where shot was token.

Circle number for a made shot.

INDIVUAL PLAYER TRACKING

Place O for a made shot.

Place X for a missed shot.

Basketball Stat Tracker

VISITORS	
HOME	
LOCATION	

SCORE	
HALF	
FINAL	

DATE

#	PLAYER	FLS		2-POINT FG		3-POINT FG		FREE THROW		REBOUND		AST	TO	STL	BLK	TOTAL POINTS
				ATT	MADE	ATT	MADE	ATT	MADE	OFF	DEF					
		1 2 3 4 5	1 2													
		1 2 3 4 5	1 2													
		1 2 3 4 5	1 2													
		1 2 3 4 5	1 2													
		1 2 3 4 5	1 2													
		1 2 3 4 5	1 2													
		1 2 3 4 5	1 2													
		1 2 3 4 5	1 2													
		1 2 3 4 5	1 2													
		1 2 3 4 5	1 2													
		1 2 3 4 5	1 2													
		1 2 3 4 5	1 2													
		1 2 3 4 5	1 2													
TEAM TOTALS																

Basketball Stat Tracker

MULTIPLE PLAYER TRACKING	INDIVUAL PLAYER TRACKING
Write number of player where shot was token. Circle number for a made shot.	Place O for a made shot. Place X for a missed shot.

Basketball Stat Tracker

VISITORS	
HOME	
LOCATION	

SCORE	
HALF	
FINAL	

DATE

#	PLAYER	FLS	2-POINT FG		3-POINT FG		FREE THROW		REBOUND		AST	TO	STL	BLK	TOTAL POINTS
			ATT	MADE	ATT	MADE	ATT	MADE	OFF	DEF					
		1 2 3 / 4 5	1 / 2												
		1 2 3 / 4 5	1 / 2												
		1 2 3 / 4 5	1 / 2												
		1 2 3 / 4 5	1 / 2												
		1 2 3 / 4 5	1 / 2												
		1 2 3 / 4 5	1 / 2												
		1 2 3 / 4 5	1 / 2												
		1 2 3 / 4 5	1 / 2												
		1 2 3 / 4 5	1 / 2												
		1 2 3 / 4 5	1 / 2												
		1 2 3 / 4 5	1 / 2												
		1 2 3 / 4 5	1 / 2												
		1 2 3 / 4 5	1 / 2												
	TEAM TOTALS														

Basketball Stat Tracker

MULTIPLE PLAYER TRACKING	INDIVUAL PLAYER TRACKING
Write number of player where shot was token. Circle number for a made shot.	Place O for a made shot. Place X for a missed shot.

Basketball Stat Tracker

VISITORS	
HOME	
LOCATION	

SCORE	
HALF	
FINAL	

DATE

#	PLAYER	FLS	2-POINT FG		3-POINT FG		FREE THROW		REBOUND		AST	TO	STL	BLK	TOTAL POINTS
			ATT	MADE	ATT	MADE	ATT	MADE	OFF	DEF					
		1 2 3 / 4 5 / 1 2													
		1 2 3 / 4 5 / 1 2													
		1 2 3 / 4 5 / 1 2													
		1 2 3 / 4 5 / 1 2													
		1 2 3 / 4 5 / 1 2													
		1 2 3 / 4 5 / 1 2													
		1 2 3 / 4 5 / 1 2													
		1 2 3 / 4 5 / 1 2													
		1 2 3 / 4 5 / 1 2													
		1 2 3 / 4 5 / 1 2													
		1 2 3 / 4 5 / 1 2													
		1 2 3 / 4 5 / 1 2													
		1 2 3 / 4 5 / 1 2													
		1 2 3 / 4 5 / 1 2													
	TEAM TOTALS														

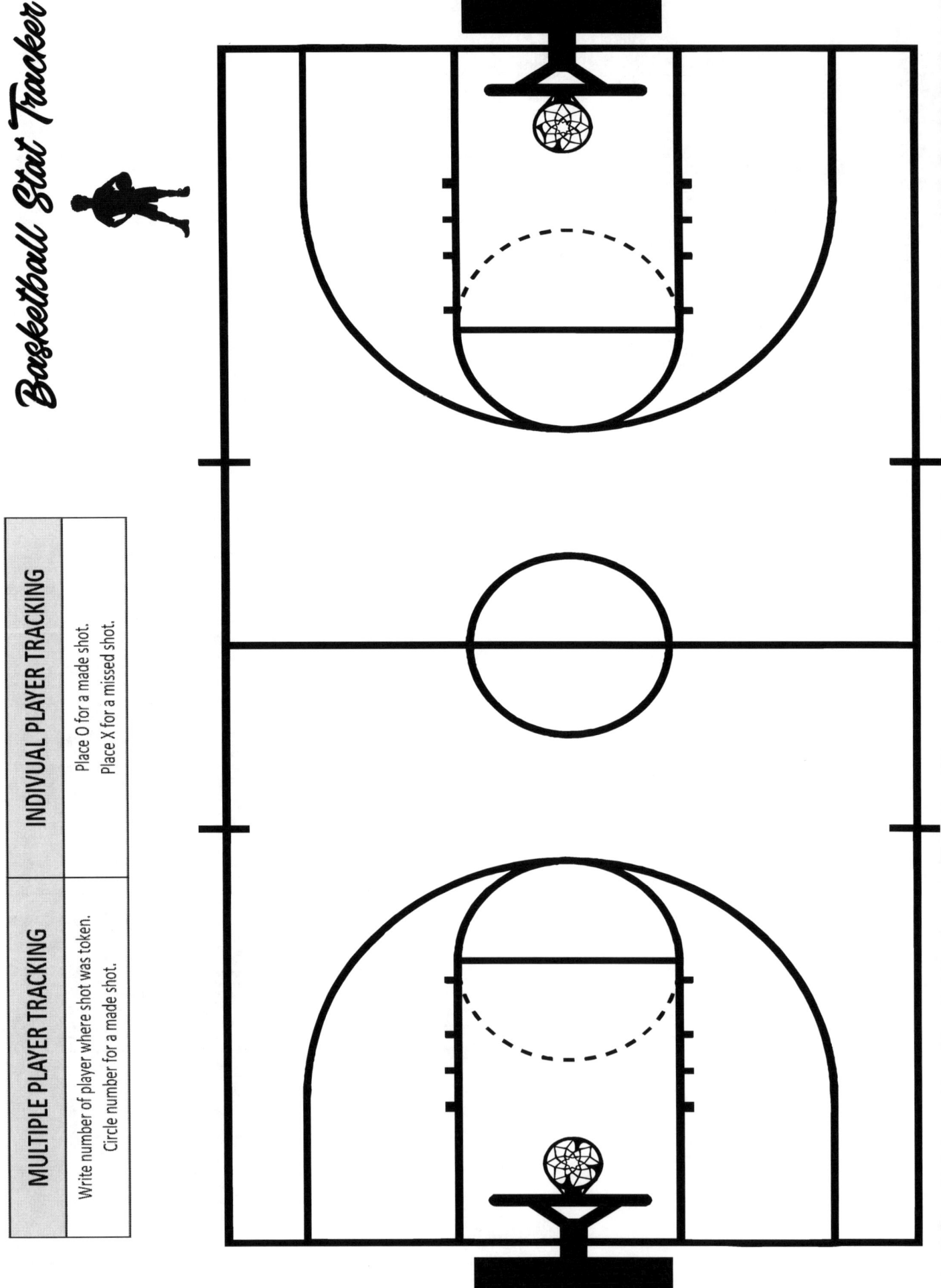

Basketball Stat Tracker

MULTIPLE PLAYER TRACKING

Write number of player where shot was token.

Circle number for a made shot.

INDIVUAL PLAYER TRACKING

Place O for a made shot.

Place X for a missed shot.

Basketball Stat Tracker

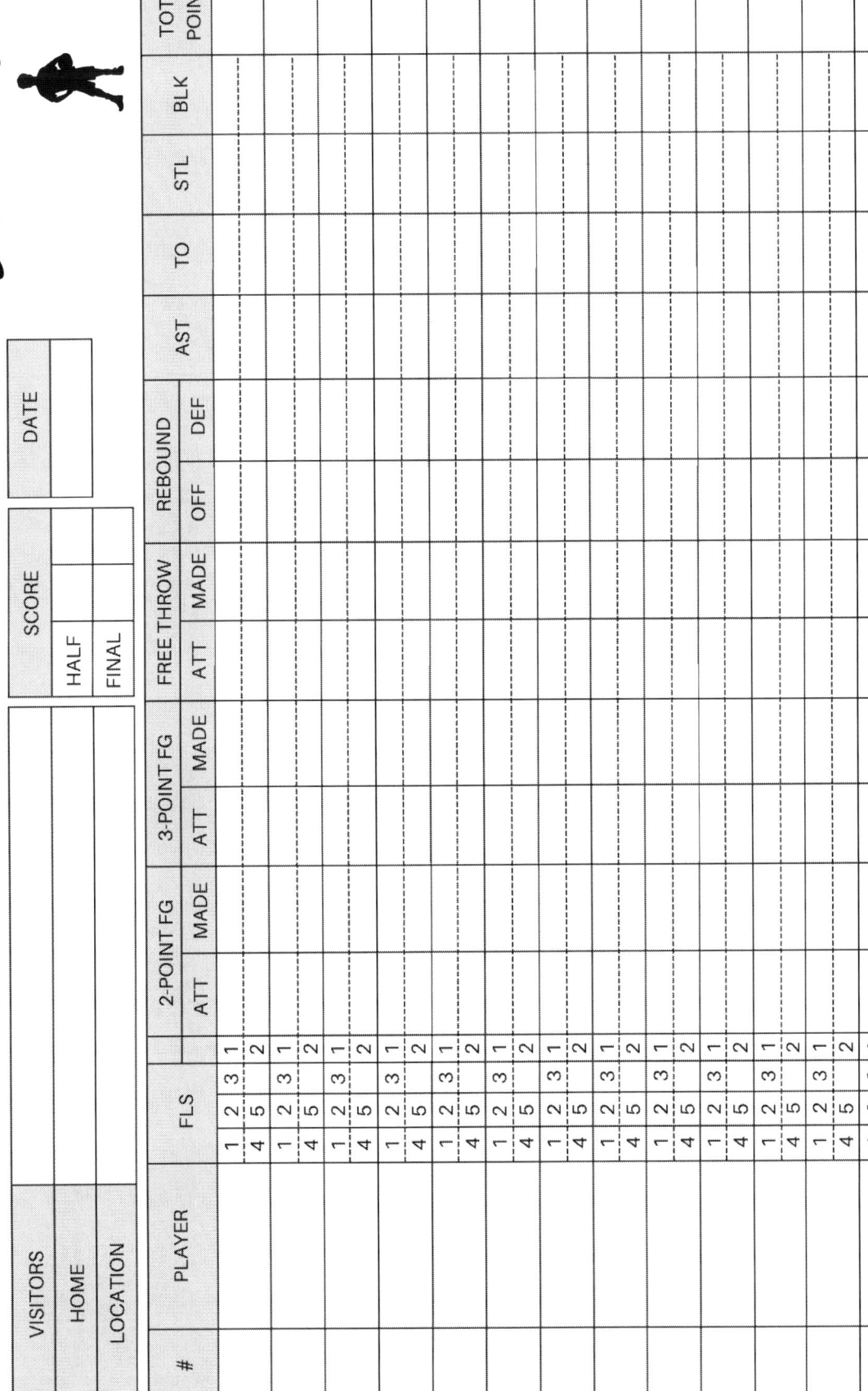

VISITORS	
HOME	
LOCATION	

SCORE	
HALF	
FINAL	

DATE

#	PLAYER	FLS				2-POINT FG		3-POINT FG		FREE THROW		REBOUND		AST	TO	STL	BLK	TOTAL POINTS
						ATT	MADE	ATT	MADE	ATT	MADE	OFF	DEF					
		1	2	3	1													
		4	5		2													
		1	2	3	1													
		4	5		2													
		1	2	3	1													
		4	5		2													
		1	2	3	1													
		4	5		2													
		1	2	3	1													
		4	5		2													
		1	2	3	1													
		4	5		2													
		1	2	3	1													
		4	5		2													
		1	2	3	1													
		4	5		2													
		1	2	3	1													
		4	5		2													
		1	2	3	1													
		4	5		2													
		1	2	3	1													
		4	5		2													
		1	2	3	1													
		4	5		2													
TEAM TOTALS																		

Basketball Stat Tracker

MULTIPLE PLAYER TRACKING	INDIVUAL PLAYER TRACKING
Write number of player where shot was taken.	Place O for a made shot.
Circle number for a made shot.	Place X for a missed shot.

Basketball Stat Tracker

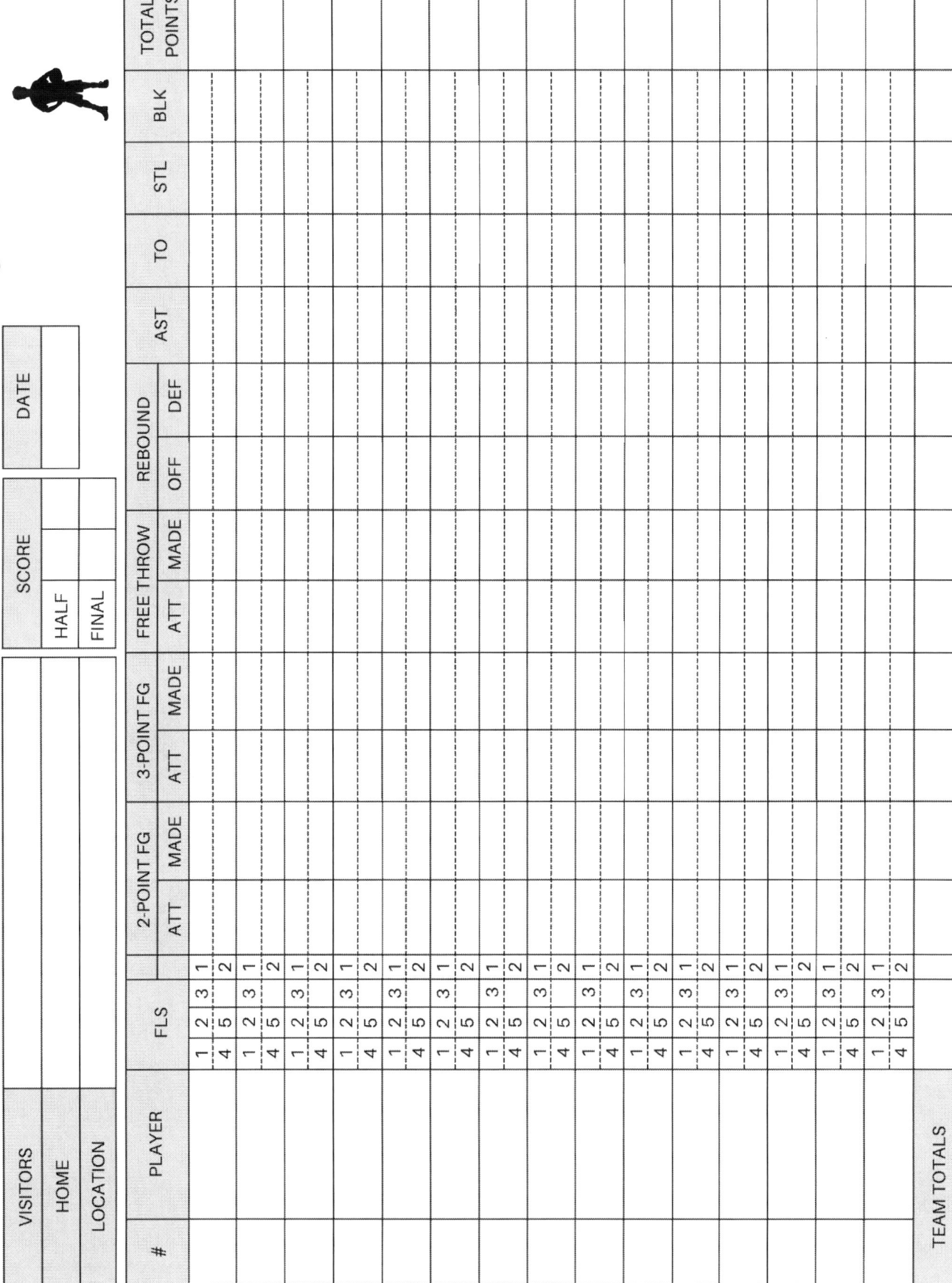

VISITORS	
HOME	
LOCATION	

SCORE	
HALF	
FINAL	

DATE

#	PLAYER	FLS		2-POINT FG		3-POINT FG		FREE THROW		REBOUND		AST	TO	STL	BLK	TOTAL POINTS
				ATT	MADE	ATT	MADE	ATT	MADE	OFF	DEF					
		1 2 3 / 4 5	1 2													
		1 2 3 / 4 5	1 2													
		1 2 3 / 4 5	1 2													
		1 2 3 / 4 5	1 2													
		1 2 3 / 4 5	1 2													
		1 2 3 / 4 5	1 2													
		1 2 3 / 4 5	1 2													
		1 2 3 / 4 5	1 2													
		1 2 3 / 4 5	1 2													
		1 2 3 / 4 5	1 2													
		1 2 3 / 4 5	1 2													
		1 2 3 / 4 5	1 2													
		1 2 3 / 4 5	1 2													
		1 2 3 / 4 5	1 2													
	TEAM TOTALS															

Basketball Stat Tracker

MULTIPLE PLAYER TRACKING	INDIVUAL PLAYER TRACKING
Write number of player where shot was token. Circle number for a made shot.	Place O for a made shot. Place X for a missed shot.

Basketball Stat Tracker

VISITORS	
HOME	
LOCATION	

SCORE	
HALF	
FINAL	

DATE

#	PLAYER	FLS	2-POINT FG		3-POINT FG		FREE THROW		REBOUND		AST	TO	STL	BLK	TOTAL POINTS
		1 2 3 / 1 2	ATT	MADE	ATT	MADE	ATT	MADE	OFF	DEF					
		4 5 / 2													
		1 2 3 / 1 2													
		4 5 / 2													
		1 2 3 / 1 2													
		4 5 / 2													
		1 2 3 / 1 2													
		4 5 / 2													
		1 2 3 / 1 2													
		4 5 / 2													
		1 2 3 / 1 2													
		4 5 / 2													
		1 2 3 / 1 2													
		4 5 / 2													
		1 2 3 / 1 2													
		4 5 / 2													
		1 2 3 / 1 2													
		4 5 / 2													
		1 2 3 / 1 2													
		4 5 / 2													
		1 2 3 / 1 2													
		4 5 / 2													
		1 2 3 / 1 2													
		4 5 / 2													
TEAM TOTALS															

Basketball Stat Tracker

MULTIPLE PLAYER TRACKING

Write number of player where shot was token.
Circle number for a made shot.

INDIVUAL PLAYER TRACKING

Place O for a made shot.
Place X for a missed shot.

Basketball Stat Tracker

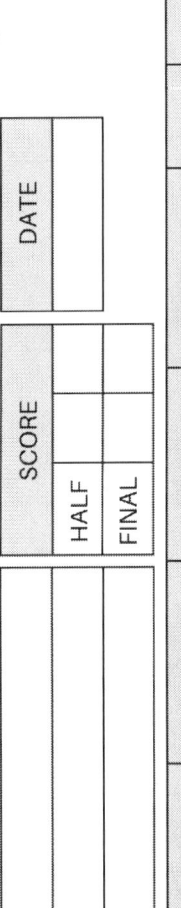

VISITORS	
HOME	
LOCATION	

SCORE	
HALF	
FINAL	

DATE

#	PLAYER	FLS			2-POINT FG		3-POINT FG		FREE THROW		REBOUND		AST	TO	STL	BLK	TOTAL POINTS
---	---	---	---	---	ATT	MADE	ATT	MADE	ATT	MADE	OFF	DEF					
		1 2 3	4 5	1 2													
		1 2 3	4 5	1 2													
		1 2 3	4 5	1 2													
		1 2 3	4 5	1 2													
		1 2 3	4 5	1 2													
		1 2 3	4 5	1 2													
		1 2 3	4 5	1 2													
		1 2 3	4 5	1 2													
		1 2 3	4 5	1 2													
		1 2 3	4 5	1 2													
		1 2 3	4 5	1 2													
		1 2 3	4 5	1 2													
		1 2 3	4 5	1 2													
		1 2 3	4 5	1 2													
	TEAM TOTALS																

Basketball Stat Tracker

MULTIPLE PLAYER TRACKING	INDIVUAL PLAYER TRACKING
Write number of player where shot was token. Circle number for a made shot.	Place O for a made shot. Place X for a missed shot.

Basketball Stat Tracker

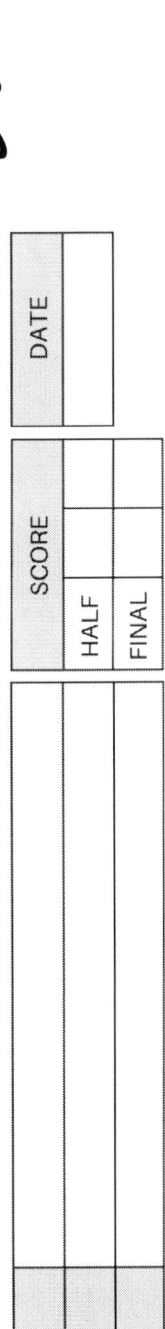

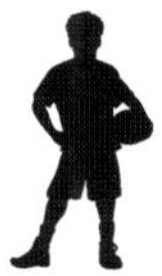

VISITORS		SCORE			DATE
HOME		HALF			
LOCATION		FINAL			

#	PLAYER	FLS		2-POINT FG		3-POINT FG		FREE THROW		REBOUND		AST	TO	STL	BLK	TOTAL POINTS
				ATT	MADE	ATT	MADE	ATT	MADE	OFF	DEF					
		1 2 3 4 5	1 2													
		1 2 3 4 5	1 2													
		1 2 3 4 5	1 2													
		1 2 3 4 5	1 2													
		1 2 3 4 5	1 2													
		1 2 3 4 5	1 2													
		1 2 3 4 5	1 2													
		1 2 3 4 5	1 2													
		1 2 3 4 5	1 2													
		1 2 3 4 5	1 2													
		1 2 3 4 5	1 2													
		1 2 3 4 5	1 2													
		1 2 3 4 5	1 2													
		1 2 3 4 5	1 2													
		1 2 3 4 5	1 2													
TEAM TOTALS																

Basketball Stat Tracker

MULTIPLE PLAYER TRACKING	INDIVUAL PLAYER TRACKING
Write number of player where shot was token. Circle number for a made shot.	Place O for a made shot. Place X for a missed shot.

Basketball Stat Tracker

VISITORS	
HOME	
LOCATION	

SCORE	
HALF	
FINAL	

DATE

#	PLAYER	FLS		2-POINT FG		3-POINT FG		FREE THROW		REBOUND		AST	TO	STL	BLK	TOTAL POINTS
				ATT	MADE	ATT	MADE	ATT	MADE	OFF	DEF					
		1 2 3 4 5	1 2													
		1 2 3 4 5	1 2													
		1 2 3 4 5	1 2													
		1 2 3 4 5	1 2													
		1 2 3 4 5	1 2													
		1 2 3 4 5	1 2													
		1 2 3 4 5	1 2													
		1 2 3 4 5	1 2													
		1 2 3 4 5	1 2													
		1 2 3 4 5	1 2													
		1 2 3 4 5	1 2													
		1 2 3 4 5	1 2													
		1 2 3 4 5	1 2													
		1 2 3 4 5	1 2													
TEAM TOTALS																

Basketball Stat Tracker

MULTIPLE PLAYER TRACKING	INDIVUAL PLAYER TRACKING
Write number of player where shot was token.	Place O for a made shot.
Circle number for a made shot.	Place X for a missed shot.

Basketball Stat Tracker

VISITORS	
HOME	
LOCATION	

SCORE	
HALF	
FINAL	

DATE

#	PLAYER	FLS		2-POINT FG		3-POINT FG		FREE THROW		REBOUND		AST	TO	STL	BLK	TOTAL POINTS
				ATT	MADE	ATT	MADE	ATT	MADE	OFF	DEF					
		1 2 3 4 5	1 2													
		1 2 3 4 5	1 2													
		1 2 3 4 5	1 2													
		1 2 3 4 5	1 2													
		1 2 3 4 5	1 2													
		1 2 3 4 5	1 2													
		1 2 3 4 5	1 2													
		1 2 3 4 5	1 2													
		1 2 3 4 5	1 2													
		1 2 3 4 5	1 2													
		1 2 3 4 5	1 2													
		1 2 3 4 5	1 2													
		1 2 3 4 5	1 2													
		1 2 3 4 5	1 2													
	TEAM TOTALS															

Basketball Stat Tracker

MULTIPLE PLAYER TRACKING

Write number of player where shot was token.
Circle number for a made shot.

INDIVUAL PLAYER TRACKING

Place O for a made shot.
Place X for a missed shot.

Basketball Stat Tracker

VISITORS	
HOME	
LOCATION	

SCORE	
HALF	
FINAL	

DATE

#	PLAYER	FLS		2-POINT FG		3-POINT FG		FREE THROW		REBOUND		AST	TO	STL	BLK	TOTAL POINTS
				ATT	MADE	ATT	MADE	ATT	MADE	OFF	DEF					
		1 2 3 4 5	1 2													
		1 2 3 4 5	1 2													
		1 2 3 4 5	1 2													
		1 2 3 4 5	1 2													
		1 2 3 4 5	1 2													
		1 2 3 4 5	1 2													
		1 2 3 4 5	1 2													
		1 2 3 4 5	1 2													
		1 2 3 4 5	1 2													
		1 2 3 4 5	1 2													
		1 2 3 4 5	1 2													
		1 2 3 4 5	1 2													
		1 2 3 4 5	1 2													
		1 2 3 4 5	1 2													
		1 2 3 4 5	1 2													
	TEAM TOTALS															

Basketball Stat Tracker

MULTIPLE PLAYER TRACKING	INDIVUAL PLAYER TRACKING
Write number of player where shot was taken. Circle number for a made shot.	Place O for a made shot. Place X for a missed shot.

Basketball Stat Tracker

VISITORS	
HOME	
LOCATION	

SCORE	
HALF	
FINAL	

DATE	

#	PLAYER	FLS		2-POINT FG		3-POINT FG		FREE THROW		REBOUND		AST	TO	STL	BLK	TOTAL POINTS
				ATT	MADE	ATT	MADE	ATT	MADE	OFF	DEF					
		1 2 3 / 4 5 1														
		1 2 3 / 4 5 2														
		1 2 3 / 4 5 1														
		1 2 3 / 4 5 2														
		1 2 3 / 4 5 1														
		1 2 3 / 4 5 2														
		1 2 3 / 4 5 1														
		1 2 3 / 4 5 2														
		1 2 3 / 4 5 1														
		1 2 3 / 4 5 2														
		1 2 3 / 4 5 1														
		1 2 3 / 4 5 2														
		1 2 3 / 4 5 1														
		1 2 3 / 4 5 2														
		1 2 3 / 4 5 1														
		1 2 3 / 4 5 2														
		1 2 3 / 4 5 1														
		1 2 3 / 4 5 2														
		1 2 3 / 4 5 1														
		1 2 3 / 4 5 2														
		1 2 3 / 4 5 1														
		1 2 3 / 4 5 2														
		1 2 3 / 4 5 1														
		1 2 3 / 4 5 2														
	TEAM TOTALS															

Basketball Stat Tracker

MULTIPLE PLAYER TRACKING	INDIVUAL PLAYER TRACKING
Write number of player where shot was token. Circle number for a made shot.	Place O for a made shot. Place X for a missed shot.

Basketball Stat Tracker

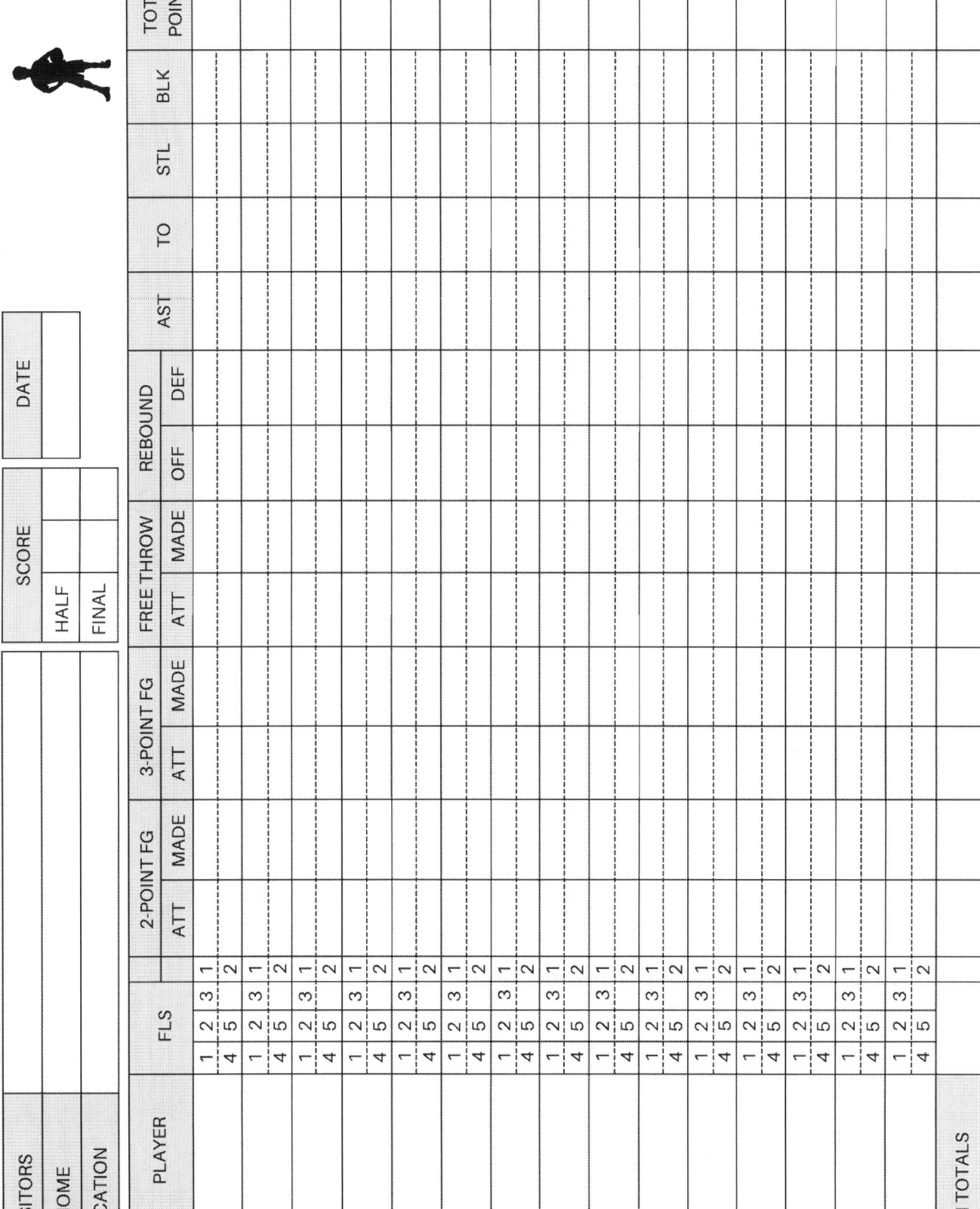

VISITORS	
HOME	
LOCATION	

SCORE	
HALF	
FINAL	

DATE	

#	PLAYER	FLS		2-POINT FG		3-POINT FG		FREE THROW		REBOUND		AST	TO	STL	BLK	TOTAL POINTS
				ATT	MADE	ATT	MADE	ATT	MADE	OFF	DEF					
		1 2 3 / 4 5	1 / 2													
		1 2 3 / 4 5	1 / 2													
		1 2 3 / 4 5	1 / 2													
		1 2 3 / 4 5	1 / 2													
		1 2 3 / 4 5	1 / 2													
		1 2 3 / 4 5	1 / 2													
		1 2 3 / 4 5	1 / 2													
		1 2 3 / 4 5	1 / 2													
		1 2 3 / 4 5	1 / 2													
		1 2 3 / 4 5	1 / 2													
		1 2 3 / 4 5	1 / 2													
		1 2 3 / 4 5	1 / 2													
		1 2 3 / 4 5	1 / 2													
		1 2 3 / 4 5	1 / 2													
		1 2 3 / 4 5	1 / 2													
	TEAM TOTALS															

Basketball Stat Tracker

MULTIPLE PLAYER TRACKING	INDIVUAL PLAYER TRACKING
Write number of player where shot was token.	Place O for a made shot.
Circle number for a made shot.	Place X for a missed shot.

Basketball Stat Tracker

VISITORS	
HOME	
LOCATION	

DATE	

SCORE	
HALF	
FINAL	

#	PLAYER	FLS		2-POINT FG		3-POINT FG		FREE THROW		REBOUND		AST	TO	STL	BLK	TOTAL POINTS
				ATT	MADE	ATT	MADE	ATT	MADE	OFF	DEF					
		1 2 3 4 5	1 2													
		1 2 3 4 5	1 2													
		1 2 3 4 5	1 2													
		1 2 3 4 5	1 2													
		1 2 3 4 5	1 2													
		1 2 3 4 5	1 2													
		1 2 3 4 5	1 2													
		1 2 3 4 5	1 2													
		1 2 3 4 5	1 2													
		1 2 3 4 5	1 2													
		1 2 3 4 5	1 2													
		1 2 3 4 5	1 2													
		1 2 3 4 5	1 2													
		1 2 3 4 5	1 2													
		1 2 3 4 5	1 2													
	TEAM TOTALS															

Basketball Stat Tracker

MULTIPLE PLAYER TRACKING	INDIVUAL PLAYER TRACKING
Write number of player where shot was token. Circle number for a made shot.	Place O for a made shot. Place X for a missed shot.

Basketball Stat Tracker

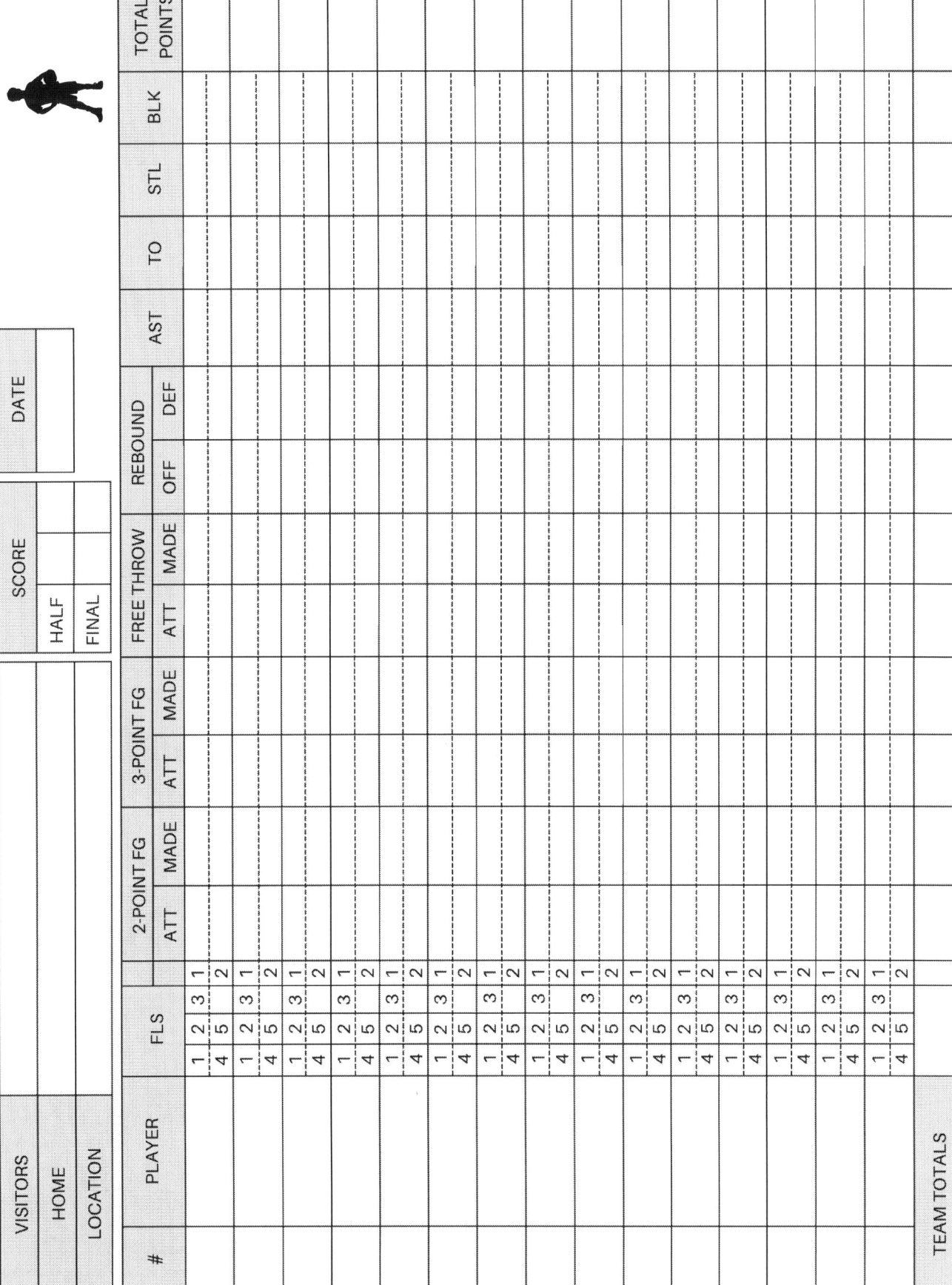

VISITORS		
HOME		
LOCATION		

SCORE			DATE
HALF			
FINAL			

#	PLAYER	FLS	2-POINT FG ATT	2-POINT FG MADE	3-POINT FG ATT	3-POINT FG MADE	FREE THROW ATT	FREE THROW MADE	REBOUND OFF	REBOUND DEF	AST	TO	STL	BLK	TOTAL POINTS
		1 2 3 / 1 4 5 / 2													
		1 2 3 / 1 4 5 / 2													
		1 2 3 / 1 4 5 / 2													
		1 2 3 / 1 4 5 / 2													
		1 2 3 / 1 4 5 / 2													
		1 2 3 / 1 4 5 / 2													
		1 2 3 / 1 4 5 / 2													
		1 2 3 / 1 4 5 / 2													
		1 2 3 / 1 4 5 / 2													
		1 2 3 / 1 4 5 / 2													
		1 2 3 / 1 4 5 / 2													
		1 2 3 / 1 4 5 / 2													
		1 2 3 / 1 4 5 / 2													
	TEAM TOTALS														

Basketball Stat Tracker

MULTIPLE PLAYER TRACKING

Write number of player where shot was token.

Circle number for a made shot.

INDIVUAL PLAYER TRACKING

Place O for a made shot.

Place X for a missed shot.

Basketball Stat Tracker

VISITORS	
HOME	
LOCATION	

SCORE	
HALF	
FINAL	

DATE	

#	PLAYER	FLS	2-POINT FG		3-POINT FG		FREE THROW		REBOUND		AST	TO	STL	BLK	TOTAL POINTS
			ATT	MADE	ATT	MADE	ATT	MADE	OFF	DEF					
		1 2 3 4 5	1 2												
		1 2 3 4 5	1 2												
		1 2 3 4 5	1 2												
		1 2 3 4 5	1 2												
		1 2 3 4 5	1 2												
		1 2 3 4 5	1 2												
		1 2 3 4 5	1 2												
		1 2 3 4 5	1 2												
		1 2 3 4 5	1 2												
		1 2 3 4 5	1 2												
		1 2 3 4 5	1 2												
		1 2 3 4 5	1 2												
		1 2 3 4 5	1 2												
		1 2 3 4 5	1 2												
		1 2 3 4 5	1 2												
	TEAM TOTALS														

Basketball Stat Tracker

MULTIPLE PLAYER TRACKING	INDIVUAL PLAYER TRACKING
Write number of player where shot was taken. Circle number for a made shot.	Place O for a made shot. Place X for a missed shot.

Basketball Stat Tracker

VISITORS	
HOME	
LOCATION	

SCORE	
HALF	
FINAL	

DATE

#	PLAYER	FLS		2-POINT FG		3-POINT FG		FREE THROW		REBOUND		AST	TO	STL	BLK	TOTAL POINTS
				ATT	MADE	ATT	MADE	ATT	MADE	OFF	DEF					
		1 2 3 4 5	1 2													
		1 2 3 4 5	1 2													
		1 2 3 4 5	1 2													
		1 2 3 4 5	1 2													
		1 2 3 4 5	1 2													
		1 2 3 4 5	1 2													
		1 2 3 4 5	1 2													
		1 2 3 4 5	1 2													
		1 2 3 4 5	1 2													
		1 2 3 4 5	1 2													
		1 2 3 4 5	1 2													
		1 2 3 4 5	1 2													
		1 2 3 4 5	1 2													
		1 2 3 4 5	1 2													
	TEAM TOTALS															

Basketball Stat Tracker

MULTIPLE PLAYER TRACKING

Write number of player where shot was token.

Circle number for a made shot.

INDIVUAL PLAYER TRACKING

Place O for a made shot.

Place X for a missed shot.

Basketball Stat Tracker

VISITORS	
HOME	
LOCATION	

SCORE	
HALF	
FINAL	

DATE

#	PLAYER	FLS	2-POINT FG		3-POINT FG		FREE THROW		REBOUND		AST	TO	STL	BLK	TOTAL POINTS
			ATT	MADE	ATT	MADE	ATT	MADE	OFF	DEF					
		1 2 3 / 4 5 / 1 2													
		1 2 3 / 4 5 / 1 2													
		1 2 3 / 4 5 / 1 2													
		1 2 3 / 4 5 / 1 2													
		1 2 3 / 4 5 / 1 2													
		1 2 3 / 4 5 / 1 2													
		1 2 3 / 4 5 / 1 2													
		1 2 3 / 4 5 / 1 2													
		1 2 3 / 4 5 / 1 2													
		1 2 3 / 4 5 / 1 2													
		1 2 3 / 4 5 / 1 2													
		1 2 3 / 4 5 / 1 2													
		1 2 3 / 4 5 / 1 2													
		1 2 3 / 4 5 / 1 2													
		1 2 3 / 4 5 / 1 2													
	TEAM TOTALS														

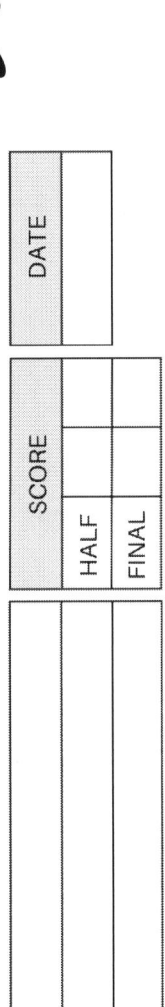

Basketball Stat Tracker

MULTIPLE PLAYER TRACKING	INDIVUAL PLAYER TRACKING
Write number of player where shot was token. Circle number for a made shot.	Place O for a made shot. Place X for a missed shot.

Basketball Stat Tracker

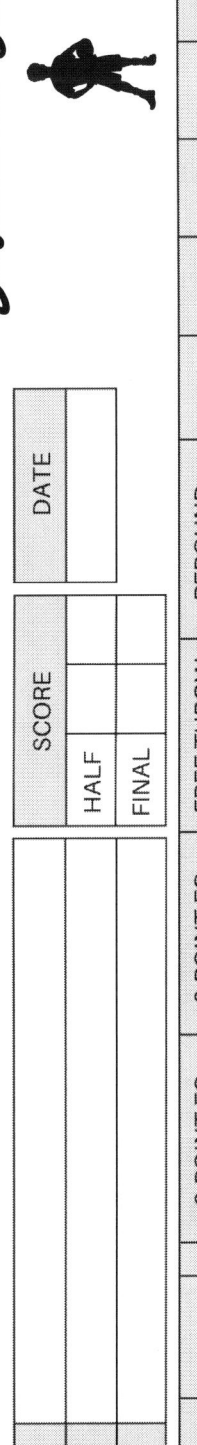

VISITORS		SCORE	DATE
HOME		HALF	
LOCATION		FINAL	

#	PLAYER	FLS		2-POINT FG		3-POINT FG		FREE THROW		REBOUND		AST	TO	STL	BLK	TOTAL POINTS
				ATT	MADE	ATT	MADE	ATT	MADE	OFF	DEF					
		1 2 3 4 5	1 2													
		1 2 3 4 5	1 2													
		1 2 3 4 5	1 2													
		1 2 3 4 5	1 2													
		1 2 3 4 5	1 2													
		1 2 3 4 5	1 2													
		1 2 3 4 5	1 2													
		1 2 3 4 5	1 2													
		1 2 3 4 5	1 2													
		1 2 3 4 5	1 2													
		1 2 3 4 5	1 2													
		1 2 3 4 5	1 2													
		1 2 3 4 5	1 2													
		1 2 3 4 5	1 2													
		1 2 3 4 5	1 2													
TEAM TOTALS																

Basketball Stat Tracker

MULTIPLE PLAYER TRACKING	INDIVUAL PLAYER TRACKING
Write number of player where shot was token. Circle number for a made shot.	Place O for a made shot. Place X for a missed shot.

Basketball Stat Tracker

VISITORS	
HOME	
LOCATION	

SCORE	
HALF	
FINAL	

DATE

#	PLAYER	FLS	2-POINT FG		3-POINT FG		FREE THROW		REBOUND		AST	TO	STL	BLK	TOTAL POINTS
			ATT	MADE	ATT	MADE	ATT	MADE	OFF	DEF					
		1 2 3 1 4 5 2													
		1 2 3 1 4 5 2													
		1 2 3 1 4 5 2													
		1 2 3 1 4 5 2													
		1 2 3 1 4 5 2													
		1 2 3 1 4 5 2													
		1 2 3 1 4 5 2													
		1 2 3 1 4 5 2													
		1 2 3 1 4 5 2													
		1 2 3 1 4 5 2													
		1 2 3 1 4 5 2													
		1 2 3 1 4 5 2													
		1 2 3 1 4 5 2													
		1 2 3 1 4 5 2													
	TEAM TOTALS														

Basketball Stat Tracker

MULTIPLE PLAYER TRACKING	INDIVUAL PLAYER TRACKING
Write number of player where shot was taken. Circle number for a made shot.	Place O for a made shot. Place X for a missed shot.

Basketball Stat Tracker

VISITORS	
HOME	
LOCATION	

SCORE	
HALF	
FINAL	

DATE	

#	PLAYER	FLS	2-POINT FG ATT	2-POINT FG MADE	3-POINT FG ATT	3-POINT FG MADE	FREE THROW ATT	FREE THROW MADE	REBOUND OFF	REBOUND DEF	AST	TO	STL	BLK	TOTAL POINTS
		1 2 3 / 4 5 / 1 2													
		1 2 3 / 4 5 / 1 2													
		1 2 3 / 4 5 / 1 2													
		1 2 3 / 4 5 / 1 2													
		1 2 3 / 4 5 / 1 2													
		1 2 3 / 4 5 / 1 2													
		1 2 3 / 4 5 / 1 2													
		1 2 3 / 4 5 / 1 2													
		1 2 3 / 4 5 / 1 2													
		1 2 3 / 4 5 / 1 2													
		1 2 3 / 4 5 / 1 2													
		1 2 3 / 4 5 / 1 2													
		1 2 3 / 4 5 / 1 2													
		1 2 3 / 4 5 / 1 2													
	TEAM TOTALS														

Basketball Stat Tracker

MULTIPLE PLAYER TRACKING

Write number of player where shot was taken.

Circle number for a made shot.

INDIVUAL PLAYER TRACKING

Place O for a made shot.

Place X for a missed shot.

Basketball Stat Tracker

VISITORS	
HOME	
LOCATION	

SCORE	
HALF	
FINAL	

DATE

#	PLAYER	FLS	2-POINT FG		3-POINT FG		FREE THROW		REBOUND		AST	TO	STL	BLK	TOTAL POINTS
			ATT	MADE	ATT	MADE	ATT	MADE	OFF	DEF					
		1 2 3 / 4 5 / 1 2													
		1 2 3 / 4 5 / 1 2													
		1 2 3 / 4 5 / 1 2													
		1 2 3 / 4 5 / 1 2													
		1 2 3 / 4 5 / 1 2													
		1 2 3 / 4 5 / 1 2													
		1 2 3 / 4 5 / 1 2													
		1 2 3 / 4 5 / 1 2													
		1 2 3 / 4 5 / 1 2													
		1 2 3 / 4 5 / 1 2													
		1 2 3 / 4 5 / 1 2													
		1 2 3 / 4 5 / 1 2													
		1 2 3 / 4 5 / 1 2													
		1 2 3 / 4 5 / 1 2													
	TEAM TOTALS														

Basketball Stat Tracker

MULTIPLE PLAYER TRACKING	INDIVUAL PLAYER TRACKING
Write number of player where shot was token. Circle number for a made shot.	Place O for a made shot. Place X for a missed shot.

Basketball Stat Tracker

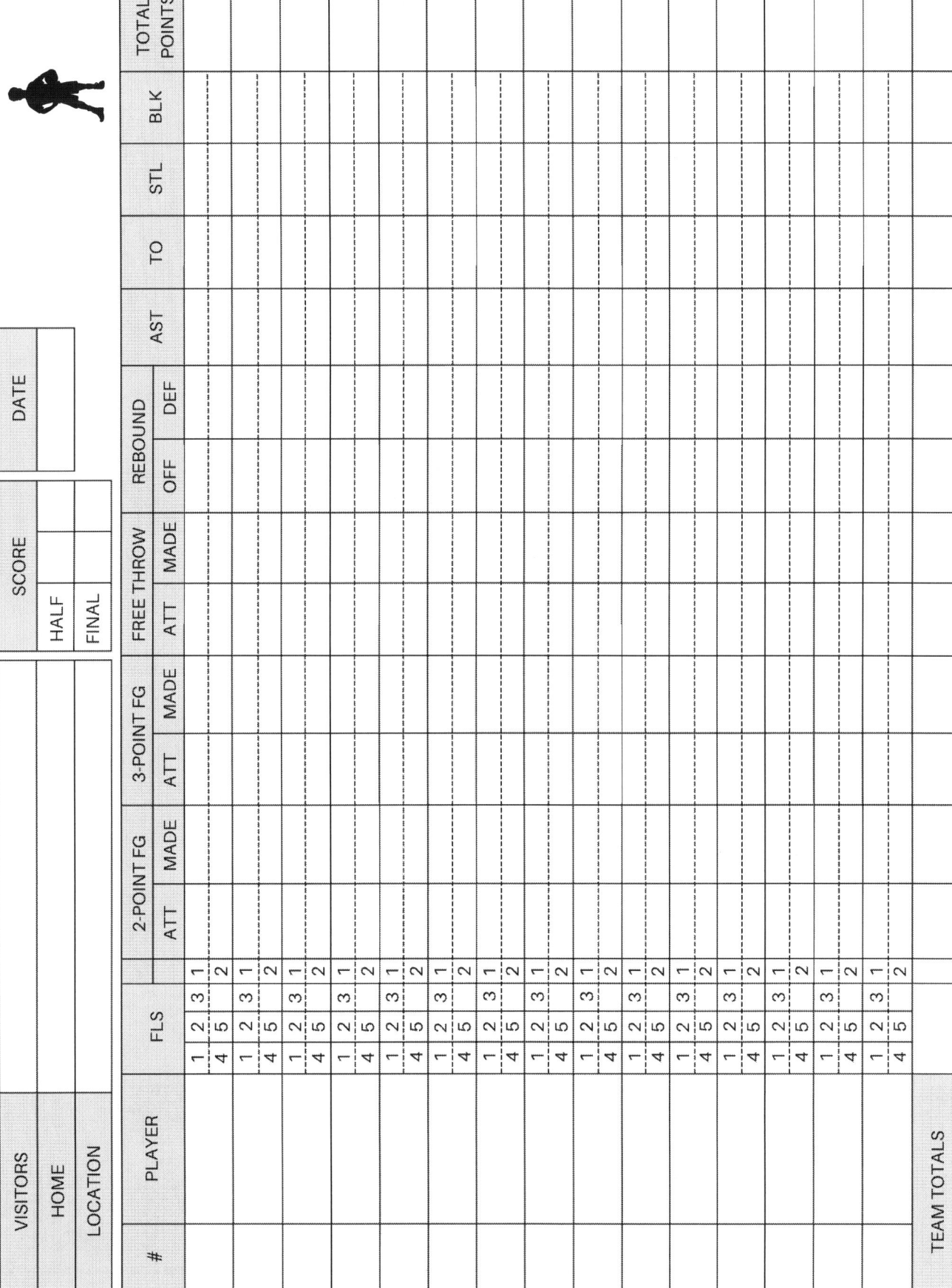

VISITORS	
HOME	
LOCATION	

SCORE	
HALF	
FINAL	

DATE

#	PLAYER	FLS			2-POINT FG		3-POINT FG		FREE THROW		REBOUND		AST	TO	STL	BLK	TOTAL POINTS
					ATT	MADE	ATT	MADE	ATT	MADE	OFF	DEF					
		1 2 3 4 5	1 2														
		1 2 3 4 5	1 2														
		1 2 3 4 5	1 2														
		1 2 3 4 5	1 2														
		1 2 3 4 5	1 2														
		1 2 3 4 5	1 2														
		1 2 3 4 5	1 2														
		1 2 3 4 5	1 2														
		1 2 3 4 5	1 2														
		1 2 3 4 5	1 2														
		1 2 3 4 5	1 2														
		1 2 3 4 5	1 2														
		1 2 3 4 5	1 2														
	TEAM TOTALS																

Basketball Stat Tracker

MULTIPLE PLAYER TRACKING

Write number of player where shot was token.

Circle number for a made shot.

INDIVUAL PLAYER TRACKING

Place O for a made shot.

Place X for a missed shot.

Basketball Stat Tracker

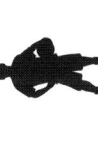

VISITORS	
HOME	
LOCATION	

SCORE		
HALF		
FINAL		

DATE

#	PLAYER	FLS		2-POINT FG		3-POINT FG		FREE THROW		REBOUND		AST	TO	STL	BLK	TOTAL POINTS
				ATT	MADE	ATT	MADE	ATT	MADE	OFF	DEF					
		1 2 3 4 5	1 2													
		1 2 3 4 5	1 2													
		1 2 3 4 5	1 2													
		1 2 3 4 5	1 2													
		1 2 3 4 5	1 2													
		1 2 3 4 5	1 2													
		1 2 3 4 5	1 2													
		1 2 3 4 5	1 2													
		1 2 3 4 5	1 2													
		1 2 3 4 5	1 2													
		1 2 3 4 5	1 2													
		1 2 3 4 5	1 2													
		1 2 3 4 5	1 2													
		1 2 3 4 5	1 2													
		1 2 3 4 5	1 2													
TEAM TOTALS																

Basketball Stat Tracker

MULTIPLE PLAYER TRACKING	INDIVUAL PLAYER TRACKING
Write number of player where shot was token. Circle number for a made shot.	Place O for a made shot. Place X for a missed shot.

Basketball Stat Tracker

VISITORS	
HOME	
LOCATION	

SCORE	
HALF	
FINAL	

DATE

#	PLAYER	FLS	2-POINT FG		3-POINT FG		FREE THROW		REBOUND		AST	TO	STL	BLK	TOTAL POINTS
			ATT	MADE	ATT	MADE	ATT	MADE	OFF	DEF					
		1 2 3 4 5 1 2													
		1 2 3 4 5 1 2													
		1 2 3 4 5 1 2													
		1 2 3 4 5 1 2													
		1 2 3 4 5 1 2													
		1 2 3 4 5 1 2													
		1 2 3 4 5 1 2													
		1 2 3 4 5 1 2													
		1 2 3 4 5 1 2													
		1 2 3 4 5 1 2													
		1 2 3 4 5 1 2													
		1 2 3 4 5 1 2													
		1 2 3 4 5 1 2													
		1 2 3 4 5 1 2													
	TEAM TOTALS														

Basketball Stat Tracker

MULTIPLE PLAYER TRACKING	INDIVIDUAL PLAYER TRACKING
Write number of player where shot was token.	Place O for a made shot.
Circle number for a made shot.	Place X for a missed shot.

Basketball Stat Tracker

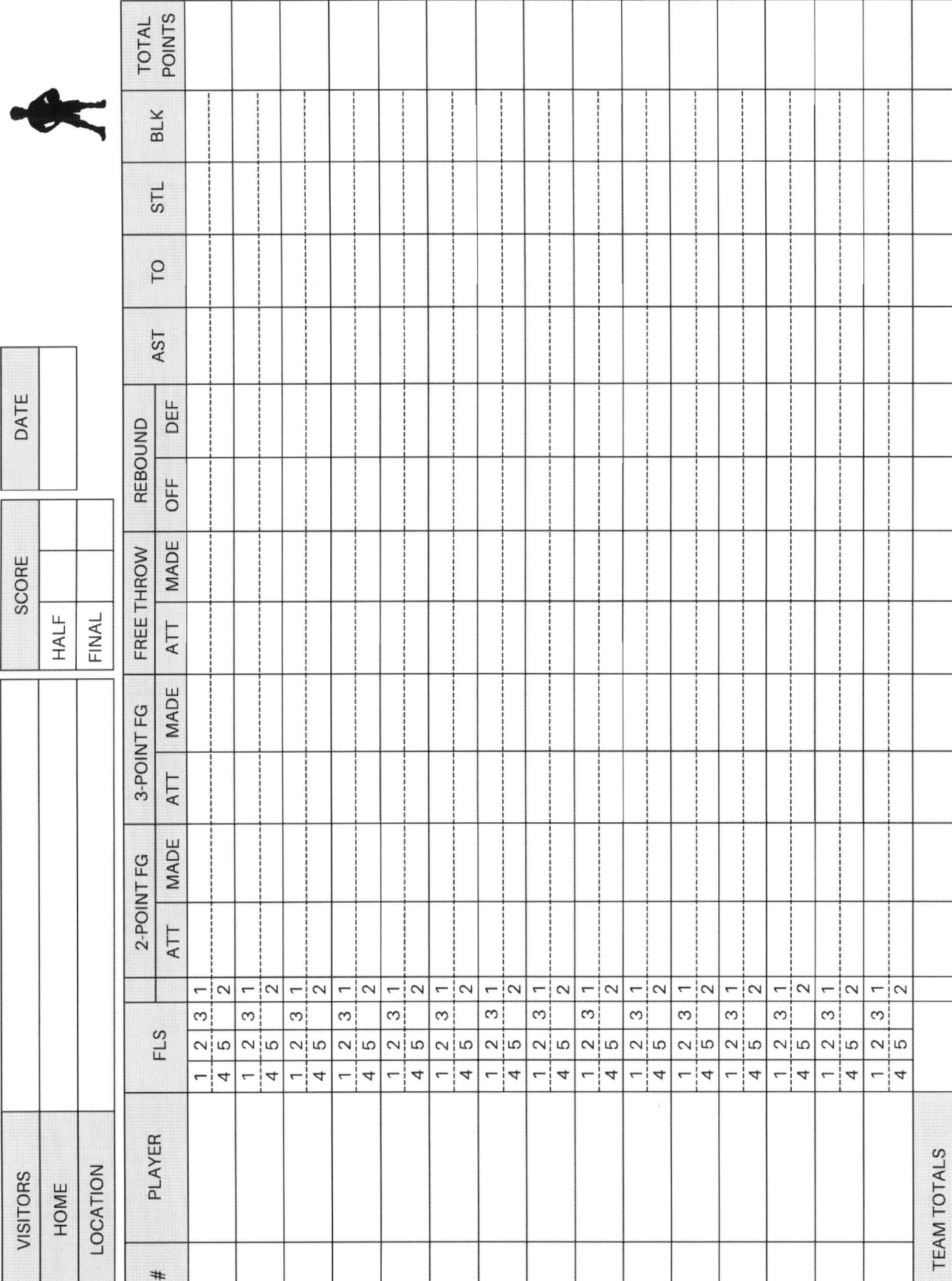

VISITORS		SCORE		DATE
HOME		HALF		
LOCATION		FINAL		

#	PLAYER	FLS		2-POINT FG		3-POINT FG		FREE THROW		REBOUND		AST	TO	STL	BLK	TOTAL POINTS
				ATT	MADE	ATT	MADE	ATT	MADE	OFF	DEF					
		1 2 3	1													
		4 5	2													
		1 2 3	1													
		4 5	2													
		1 2 3	1													
		4 5	2													
		1 2 3	1													
		4 5	2													
		1 2 3	1													
		4 5	2													
		1 2 3	1													
		4 5	2													
		1 2 3	1													
		4 5	2													
		1 2 3	1													
		4 5	2													
		1 2 3	1													
		4 5	2													
		1 2 3	1													
		4 5	2													
		1 2 3	1													
		4 5	2													
		1 2 3	1													
		4 5	2													
		1 2 3	1													
		4 5	2													
	TEAM TOTALS															

Basketball Stat Tracker

MULTIPLE PLAYER TRACKING	INDIVUAL PLAYER TRACKING
Write number of player where shot was token. Circle number for a made shot.	Place O for a made shot. Place X for a missed shot.

Basketball Stat Tracker

VISITORS	
HOME	
LOCATION	

SCORE	
HALF	
FINAL	

DATE	

#	PLAYER	FLS		2-POINT FG		3-POINT FG		FREE THROW		REBOUND		AST	TO	STL	BLK	TOTAL POINTS
				ATT	MADE	ATT	MADE	ATT	MADE	OFF	DEF					
		1 2 3 4 5	1 2													
		1 2 3 4 5	1 2													
		1 2 3 4 5	1 2													
		1 2 3 4 5	1 2													
		1 2 3 4 5	1 2													
		1 2 3 4 5	1 2													
		1 2 3 4 5	1 2													
		1 2 3 4 5	1 2													
		1 2 3 4 5	1 2													
		1 2 3 4 5	1 2													
		1 2 3 4 5	1 2													
		1 2 3 4 5	1 2													
		1 2 3 4 5	1 2													
		1 2 3 4 5	1 2													
	TEAM TOTALS															

Basketball Stat Tracker

MULTIPLE PLAYER TRACKING	INDIVUAL PLAYER TRACKING
Write number of player where shot was token. Circle number for a made shot.	Place O for a made shot. Place X for a missed shot.

Basketball Stat Tracker

VISITORS	
HOME	
LOCATION	

SCORE	
HALF	
FINAL	

DATE	

#	PLAYER	FLS			2-POINT FG		3-POINT FG		FREE THROW		REBOUND		AST	TO	STL	BLK	TOTAL POINTS
					ATT	MADE	ATT	MADE	ATT	MADE	OFF	DEF					
		1 2 3 4 5	1 2														
		1 2 3 4 5	1 2														
		1 2 3 4 5	1 2														
		1 2 3 4 5	1 2														
		1 2 3 4 5	1 2														
		1 2 3 4 5	1 2														
		1 2 3 4 5	1 2														
		1 2 3 4 5	1 2														
		1 2 3 4 5	1 2														
		1 2 3 4 5	1 2														
		1 2 3 4 5	1 2														
		1 2 3 4 5	1 2														
		1 2 3 4 5	1 2														
		1 2 3 4 5	1 2														
	TEAM TOTALS																

Basketball Stat Tracker

MULTIPLE PLAYER TRACKING	INDIVUAL PLAYER TRACKING
Write number of player where shot was token. Circle number for a made shot.	Place O for a made shot. Place X for a missed shot.

Basketball Stat Tracker

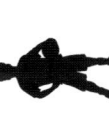

VISITORS		SCORE			DATE
HOME		HALF			
LOCATION		FINAL			

#	PLAYER	FLS		2-POINT FG		3-POINT FG		FREE THROW		REBOUND		AST	TO	STL	BLK	TOTAL POINTS
				ATT	MADE	ATT	MADE	ATT	MADE	OFF	DEF					
		1 2 3 4 5	1 2													
		1 2 3 4 5	1 2													
		1 2 3 4 5	1 2													
		1 2 3 4 5	1 2													
		1 2 3 4 5	1 2													
		1 2 3 4 5	1 2													
		1 2 3 4 5	1 2													
		1 2 3 4 5	1 2													
		1 2 3 4 5	1 2													
		1 2 3 4 5	1 2													
		1 2 3 4 5	1 2													
		1 2 3 4 5	1 2													
		1 2 3 4 5	1 2													
		1 2 3 4 5	1 2													
		1 2 3 4 5	1 2													
TEAM TOTALS																

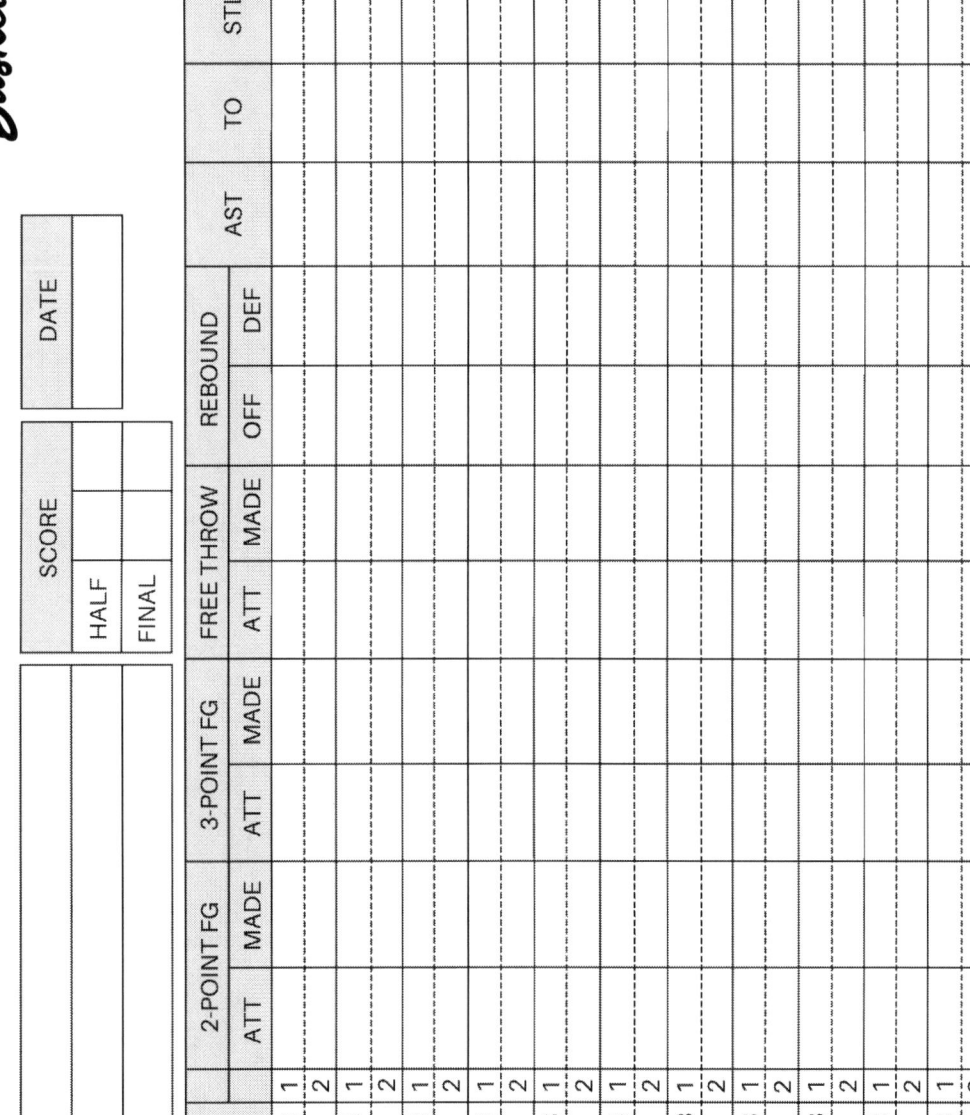

Basketball Stat Tracker

MULTIPLE PLAYER TRACKING	INDIVUAL PLAYER TRACKING
Write number of player where shot was token. Circle number for a made shot.	Place O for a made shot. Place X for a missed shot.

Basketball Stat Tracker

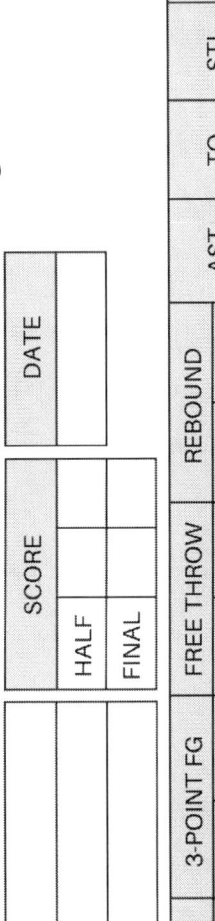

VISITORS	
HOME	
LOCATION	

SCORE		DATE	
HALF			
FINAL			

#	PLAYER	FLS	2-POINT FG		3-POINT FG		FREE THROW		REBOUND		AST	TO	STL	BLK	TOTAL POINTS
			ATT	MADE	ATT	MADE	ATT	MADE	OFF	DEF					
		1 2 3 / 4 5 / 1 2													
		1 2 3 / 4 5 / 1 2													
		1 2 3 / 4 5 / 1 2													
		1 2 3 / 4 5 / 1 2													
		1 2 3 / 4 5 / 1 2													
		1 2 3 / 4 5 / 1 2													
		1 2 3 / 4 5 / 1 2													
		1 2 3 / 4 5 / 1 2													
		1 2 3 / 4 5 / 1 2													
		1 2 3 / 4 5 / 1 2													
		1 2 3 / 4 5 / 1 2													
		1 2 3 / 4 5 / 1 2													
		1 2 3 / 4 5 / 1 2													
		1 2 3 / 4 5 / 1 2													
	TEAM TOTALS														

Basketball Stat Tracker

MULTIPLE PLAYER TRACKING	INDIVUAL PLAYER TRACKING
Write number of player where shot was token.	Place O for a made shot.
Circle number for a made shot.	Place X for a missed shot.

Basketball Stat Tracker

VISITORS	
HOME	
LOCATION	

SCORE	
HALF	
FINAL	

DATE	

#	PLAYER	FLS	2-POINT FG		3-POINT FG		FREE THROW		REBOUND		AST	TO	STL	BLK	TOTAL POINTS
			ATT	MADE	ATT	MADE	ATT	MADE	OFF	DEF					
		1 2 3 / 4 5	1 / 2												
		1 2 3 / 4 5	1 / 2												
		1 2 3 / 4 5	1 / 2												
		1 2 3 / 4 5	1 / 2												
		1 2 3 / 4 5	1 / 2												
		1 2 3 / 4 5	1 / 2												
		1 2 3 / 4 5	1 / 2												
		1 2 3 / 4 5	1 / 2												
		1 2 3 / 4 5	1 / 2												
		1 2 3 / 4 5	1 / 2												
		1 2 3 / 4 5	1 / 2												
		1 2 3 / 4 5	1 / 2												
		1 2 3 / 4 5	1 / 2												
		1 2 3 / 4 5	1 / 2												
		1 2 3 / 4 5	1 / 2												
	TEAM TOTALS														

Basketball Stat Tracker

MULTIPLE PLAYER TRACKING	INDIVUAL PLAYER TRACKING
Write number of player where shot was token. Circle number for a made shot.	Place O for a made shot. Place X for a missed shot.

Basketball Stat Tracker

VISITORS	
HOME	
LOCATION	

SCORE	
HALF	
FINAL	

DATE

#	PLAYER	FLS	2-POINT FG		3-POINT FG		FREE THROW		REBOUND		AST	TO	STL	BLK	TOTAL POINTS
		1 2 3 / 1 2 / 4 5 / 1 2	ATT	MADE	ATT	MADE	ATT	MADE	OFF	DEF					
TEAM TOTALS															

LIKE THIS BOOK ?

PLEASE LEAVE A REVIEW ON AMAZON.
THANKS!